ROBERTO CLEMENTE

ROBERTO CLEMENTE

United Press International
Text by Ira Miller, U.P.I. Sportswriter
Resumen por José M. Pérez, Periodista de U.P.I.
With a Foreword by José Torres

Tempo Books
GROSSET & DUNLAP
A National General Company
Publishers   New York

Ira Miller wishes to acknowledge the assistance of the following: Pittsburgh *Press;* Pittsburgh *Post-Gazette;* Sam Nover, sports director, WIIC-TV, Pittsburgh; Bill Guilfoile, publicity director, Pittsburgh Pirates.

FOREWORD

By José Torres
Former World's Light Heavyweight Champion

Special Representative of the Governor of
Puerto Rico in the United States

In his own life, Roberto Clemente embodied the struggle of a people. And although many of us Latin athletes felt that our struggle was more than personal, Clemente instinctively transmitted this important message to all. For he was a natural hero.

There was a time in my life when I thought that I could be a Puerto Rican hero. It was a time when Saint Nicholas Arena, Sunnyside Garden, and the different armories around New Jersey were filled with my countrymen who paid to see me knocking guys out of their senses with boxing gloves; a time when screaming Puerto Ricans fainted with excitement, cried with emotion, carried me on their shoulders after each victory, and then thanked God for my triumphs.

Then, for complicated reasons, I stopped fighting for a while. When I returned to the ring, it was to become—in 1965—the light heavyweight champion of the world. Once again Puerto Ricans carried me on their shoulders, and there was plenty of excitement. They were proud of me because I was a champ—because one of them had made it. But I was not a Puerto Rican hero. Not in the way that Clemente was.

I was a champ—and so were Carlos Ortiz in the ring and Orlando Cepeda in baseball. But it was Roberto Clemente who moved Puerto Ricans in New York and in Puerto Rico. It was Clemente who showed the Puerto Rican people that his struggle was not only their struggle, but the struggle of every other Latin human being in a strange world, the United States.

While people raved about Cepeda's home runs, Ortiz' knockouts and my peek-a-boo style, they did more than hail Roberto as a baseball superstar. They also paid attention to what he did for others in the major leagues and what he did for his people in Latin America when he was off the diamond.

So, what became the theme when we spoke about Clemente? Baseball? Well, sometimes. But many other times I heard people saying, "Why don't you join Roberto Clemente in his drive to bring a Sports City to Puerto Rico?" Or, "Why is it that New Yorkers don't know much about our great man?" This was the way we talked about him in New York and in Puerto Rico.

Roberto Clemente was deeply committed to the Sports City idea—the idea of bringing to the children of Puerto Rico a place where they could all be together and play the game of their choice. It was the subject of the last long conversation I had with him. "I need your help," he told me at the house of Felipe Rodriguez, the singer. It was my son's baptismal day, and Clemente had come to the small *fiesta* following the service.

"We can get the best people. Help me," he said. Then he went on to tell me about the mechanics of how his Sports City would work. "You and Carlos (Ortiz) can come here once in a while to motivate these kids to boxing. Orlando Cepeda and I can do the same thing for the ones who like baseball. Charley Passarell in tennis, Chichi Rodriguez in golf . . . ." And he went on through all the sports.

While his Sports City was high on Clemente's list of priorities, his interest in helping others was not limited to one idea. For many years he played winter baseball in Puerto Rico for the San Juan Senators, and he managed them for a couple of years.

I remember the time when I went to see a game between his team and the Santurce Crabbers, two traditional rivals from the San Juan metropolitan area. Orlando Cepeda was playing for the Crabbers. It was the year that Cepeda had won the Most Valuable Player Award in the majors.

Probably as a tribute to Clemente and "his" team, the first time Cepeda came to bat, there were long screaming boos. I was with Clemente in the dugout and he became so annoyed that I could see tears in his eyes. "What are they trying to do with this man?" he said angrily. "This guy is the best baseball player in the National League in the majors. What else do they want?" He got so embarrassed that he hid himself in the dugout. He thought of the people as a whole, not as fans of this team or that team.

The last time I saw him, I was in Puerto Rico campaigning for the new Governor of Puerto Rico. I was rushing to a plane and Roberto was walking back to his car, parked at the airport. "Hey Chegui," he yelled my nickname. We shook hands and I told him to give me his home telephone number. "We have to talk," I told him. I wanted him to help me campaign for Rafael Hernandez Colon. "I think that with a new Governor, we can get the Sports City," I said.

"That's fine," he said, "Call me."

When I called—months later as it turned out—it was December, 1972. He was busy on a tour around the island giving baseball clinics. "He'll be back very late tonight," his wife Vera told me. I waited a few days and I called again.

"It is going to be hard to get him at home," Vera said. "He's busy collecting clothes, medicine and money for the people in Managua, Nicaragua. Why don't you go to the baseball stadium? He's having a big marathon for the earthquake victims of Nicaragua there.

"Tell him to call me," I said.

I don't know whether he tried to call me. But two days later, at around 11:40 p.m. on the 31st of December, the biggest holiday on the island of Puerto Rico, I was told that some radio station had announced that a plane had gone down near San Juan and that Roberto Clemente was supposed to be on it. Nobody believed it, so we kept dancing. And no one mentioned it again. Many Puerto Ricans went to bed in the early morning of the first day of the New Year. And many were suddenly awakened with the news: Roberto Clemente *was* in the ill-fated DC-7 and there was no sign of the plane or of Clemente or the other four passengers.

And suddenly the Christmas spirit died in all Puerto Rico. Everyone forgot that Roberto Clemente played for the San Juan Senators. He was no longer a rival for those fans who followed the other teams in the island. Those who more than once had booed him and who had resented him when his catches or bat defeated "their" team, now got together and cried with the rest of us. Suddenly I realized that we had lost the only hero we had in Puerto Rico.

Roberto Clemente left us prematurely on a mission of good will. In the face of rumors that profiteers were getting the food, medicine and money that the Puerto Rican people were sending to the people of Nicaragua, Clemente decided that he himself would go to Managua to make sure that the right people would be helped. But he never made it on that mercy flight.

And we cried. The man who felt proud of his people and who tried to do so much for them and for others made us all cry.

For Roberto Clemente was a true superstar and not just in baseball but in the whole game of life. And in Puerto Rico and in many other places he'll also be remembered as a super Puerto Rican . . . a super human being.

New Year's Eve is a time for parties. And this particular New Year's Eve was no different. It was December 31, 1972.

Thousands of people had been killed in an earthquake only about a week earlier, destroying most of the capital city of Managua in Nicaragua. Nearly a hundred people had died 48 hours earlier in an airplane crash near Miami. But to most people, these events were distant. Unless they knew someone involved, folks tended to read the newspaper headlines and go on to another story.

So it was that in most places it was New Year's Eve as usual. And the Pittsburgh Pirates baseball players, like everyone else around the country, were celebrating.

In Pittsburgh, Steve Blass, the pitching star of the Pirates' 1971 World Series victory, was at a New Year's Eve party. He had come in from his home in Connecticut. Dave Giusti, the relief pitching ace, also was there.

Pittsburgh players Bob Johnson, Richie Zisk and Chuck Goggin were playing winter ball in Puerto Rico, but they too were celebrating. Johnson threw a party in his 27th-floor apartment overlooking the Atlantic Ocean in San Juan.

But one Pirates player was not celebrating.

Roberto Clemente, the best and the best-known of the Pirates, had announced a few days earlier that he would head up the Puerto Rican relief effort for Nicaragua. He was helping to collect clothes and food for the earthquake-torn country.

Clemente's effort rated only a few lines in most newspapers, and many people just shrugged it off. "He's just trying to get some publicity," some said. "He's not really doing anything, just letting them use his name."

These people did not know Clemente. Clemente did not let anyone "use his name." He was involved.

On New Year's Eve, in fact, Clemente was at the San Juan Airport, near Johnson's apartment, supervising the loading of supplies for Nicaragua onto an old four-engine, propeller-driven DC-7 airplane. He planned to accompany the plane to Managua and see that the goods were delivered to the proper people, before returning to Puerto Rico to celebrate New Year's himself.

"Some of the supplies were winding up in the wrong hands, on the black market," a friend was to say later. "He wanted to make sure they got to the people who needed them."

But there was trouble at the airport. The plane developed mechanical problems. The pilot was late. The takeoff was delayed a couple of times. Someone remembered that Clemente said, "If there is one more delay, we'll leave this for tomorrow."

2

Clemente's wife, Vera, was concerned that the plane seemed old and overloaded, but he told her not to worry. "What the heck, I'll go," he said. "Just be sure to have roast pork for me and the kids when I get back."

In Bob Johnson's apartment. Richie Zisk remembered: "We had heard about a plane crash.

"We saw the search crews looking for bodies and debris in the light of huge spotlights," he said. "We started to talk about how terrible it was for the people in the plane, but we had no idea what kind of a plane it was.

"We began to talk about what a terrible New Year it would be for the people who knew the victims. We watched the searchlights as one year went out and the new one came in."

Chuck Coggin said a friend of Roberto's urged him not to take the flight. Clemente is supposed to have told him, "I go now. If I die, I die."

It was 4 A.M. in Pittsburgh when the phone rang at Steve Blass and Dave Giusti's New Year's Eve party. It was Tony Bartirome, trainer of the Pirates. Bartirome had heard the news on the radio.

About this time, Joe L. Brown, General Manager of the Pirates and a friend and confidant of Clemente's, was awakened by a phone call. A little later, Blass and Giusti headed for Joe Brown's home. That was the only place they felt they should be.

The party was over. All the parties were over.

The sudden death of Roberto Clemente probably touched more people in more ways than the passing of any sports star in many years. Certainly, players come and go, careers end, players die, but not since Lou Gehrig had a star of Clemente's magnitude, still

3

in the heart of his career, been so cruelly cut down.

"If you have to die," said Pirates owner John W. Galbreath, "how better could your death be exemplified than by being on a mission of mercy? It was so typical of the man."

Typical? It was a side of Roberto Clemente very few people knew about, not even his teammates. Most of them were surprised when they learned of Clemente's work on behalf of the Nicaraguan relief effort, and most of them did not learn of it until he died.

To the public, Roberto Clemente was a many-sided, complex man.

People saw him as a hypochondriac, always complaining of injuries. "I'm fed up with the guy," Dr. Joseph Finegold, the team physician, once said when Clemente flew off to Puerto Rico for treatment by his personal physician. "If he comes to me for help again, I'm going to tell him to go back down to Puerto Rico. And I'm going to tell Joe Brown the same thing."

Yet, Joe Brown refuted the idea that Clemente was a malingerer. The trouble, Brown said, was Clemente's excellence itself. "When he is hurt," Brown observed, "he can do a lot of things better than most players can do when they are healthy. Then people wonder, 'How can he do that when he is hurt?' "

Brown recalled a time when Clemente's arm was hurt. "Clemente would grit his teeth and, once in a while, make one of his old-time throws. I'm sure if everybody knew that Clemente had a sore arm, they would be wondering how he could throw like that. But that's the way he was."

4

People also saw him as Roberto Clemente, the complainer, who whined that he never got enough recognition. In 1960, Clemente thought he should have won the National League's Most Valuable Player award: "I was the League's best player, but I didn't get a single first place vote." But the guy who won that year later made a remark—recounted in this book—that casts a much different light on Clemente's "whine." People also saw Clemente as a moody, petulant Puerto Rican.

But one thing no one could deny him was his stardom. His superb performance on the field was there for all to see. Even so, Clemente went through most of his career without the general acclaim befitting one of baseball's top talents. It was not until the 1971 World Series—after 17 years in the majors— that Clemente finally received the national acclaim from the news media that was long due. As the Series ended, Clemente said, "I finally have peace of mind."

Always there was Roberto Clemente, the human being.

Hardly anyone outside his close circle of friends knew of Clemente's charitable work, his interest in people and in children, his plans to construct a "Sports City" for Puerto Rican youth, his genuine concern for racial equality.

For instance, how many knew that he made commercials and endorsements in Puerto Rico and donated the money to charity? Or were aware that the $6,000 given him on "Roberto Clemente Night" at Three Rivers Stadium in 1970 was channeled to Children's Hospital in Pittsburgh?

Because of the controversies amid the brilliance

of Clemente's career, the public tended to be a little ambivalent on the subject of Clemente. People routinely expected great things from him, and routinely, he provided them. But he never was placed on a pedestal, immune to criticism.

One story illustrates the point.

In an exhibition game between the Pirates and their Charleston, West Virginia, farm club, Clemente played only four innings. When the game finally ended—it lasted 15 innings—people complained about Clemente as they left.

"Why, he played only four innings," said one fan. "Bet he didn't even work up a sweat."

"Yeah, and did you see him at bat? He wasn't even swinging—just going through the motions," added another.

As any fan should know full well, four innings is plenty for a superstar in a mid-season exhibition game. The players need the rest, and the manager doesn't want to wear his stars down. In Chicago in 1972, White Sox fans were thrilled when Dick Allen played just one inning in the annual exhibition game against the Cubs. But the fans tended to jump on Clemente, given an opportunity.

However, some fans in Charleston had a different perspective on Clemente when they left the ballpark that night. Jerry Deutsch, a 15-year-old Clemente fan from West Virginia who recently had been hospitalized, was at the game with a friend and with his friend's parents. While he was in the hospital, the friend's mother wrote to Clemente asking him to write a letter of encouragement to the hospitalized youth.

"He wrote him a nice letter," she said. "Then at

the game, we asked him if he'd mind meeting Jerry and our son.

"He said he would be glad to. The boys got to go into the dressing room and meet him, and he was extremely kind."

The parents said they were "happy and delighted" their son had found a hero like Clemente. "Sure, he's a temperamental man," they said, "but he's a great player, a friendly person, a good husband and a good father. What more could you ask? Things like that mean more to us as parents than all the statistics sportswriters can print."

It was a side of Roberto Clemente the average fan never saw, the casual newspaper reader never knew. It was that way because Roberto Clemente wanted it that way. When he visited hospitalized youngsters, he wanted it kept quiet. He did not want reporters or photographers following him around, and usually, he got the privacy he wanted. In what, it turned out, was Clemente's last lengthy interview —shortly after the end of the 1972 regular season— he explained why he preferred it that way.

"When you leave your life to the public, then you really have to participate in the public eye all the time," he said. "I love lots of people, but sometimes I hurt them because I cannot be with them. My first responsibility from April until October is to be in shape so I can do my best on the playing field.

"Sometimes, I cannot be with my family all I want. To me, an athlete has to be very careful about what he does. You are here for one purpose—to do the best you can in the playing months."

If the public sometimes had a complicated image of Clemente, then perhaps that was the way it should have been. He was not an easy man to type-cast.

Reporters sometimes found him gruff and grumbling but a minute later he would change beats, put on the charm, and talk as long as they wanted about anything at all.

Sure, he popped off. He always spoke what was on his mind. And he never hesitated to criticize writers, fans, umpires, managers, even teammates when he thought he was right and they were wrong.

One thing always stood out. Through the stormy outbursts, the arguments and controversies, it was almost impossible not to like the guy.

I can remember the first time as a rookie sportswriter I had to interview Clemente. There were stories that he was difficult to talk to, impossible to get close to, impatient and impolite. In other years and in other cities, writers would talk among themselves the same way about other superstars, and sometimes they were right. But I introduced myself to Clemente, and he was polite and pleasant. It was as though he sensed my own anxiety and was trying to make it easier for me.

In later years, it would not always be this way, but that, too, is as it should be. Clemente would let me know when he was displeased, and I would not hesitate to question him.

Clemente gave the impression of being a man in a hurry. After a game, he liked to dress and get out of the locker room as quickly as possible. He did not participate in clubhouse hijinx. That was not his style. But although he liked to get away quickly, he was almost always willing to sit and talk if you got to him before he walked out the door.

If the question was particularly penetrating, he

might sit there for the moment with a somewhat quizzical, little-boy look on his face, but always there was an answer. Usually it came in machine-gun rapid, heavily accented English. Always it came from his heart.

Everybody who ever came in contact with Clemente has their own favorite memories of him. All the great catches, the hits, the baseball plays tend to fade away in comparison to the personality of the man. He led the Pirates by example, not by words, but often they referred to him as "our inspiration."

It was Steve Blass, following Clemente's death, who was moved to observe that "The sad part is Pittsburgh had him so long and never really understood him.

"I think the thing that most impressed me about Roberto was that when I came to the Pirates, he was a superstar then, and he was approachable even for me—a rookie coming up," Blass said.

"When I think of excitement in baseball, I think of Roberto Clemente. His influence will remain with us for a long, long time—it doesn't seem like the Pittsburgh Pirates without Roberto Clemente."

The list of honors Clemente assembled in his career is impressive.

—He won four National League batting championships—in 1961, 1964, 1965 and 1967—and narrowly missed a couple of others—including 1968, when Pete Rose beat him out with a bunt single on the final at-bat of the season. Only six other players in all of major league history have won four or more batting titles.

—He won the National League's Most Valuable Player award in 1966.

—He batted 3,000 hits in the major leagues, a feat accomplished by only 10 other players in the nearly a century since they have been playing baseball. Lifetime batting average: .317.

—He played in more games, had more at-bats, more hits, more singles, more total bases and more runs batted in than anyone else who ever played for Pittsburgh.

—He won the Golden Glove for fielding proficiency in each of the last 12 years of his career.

—But most of all, Roberto Clemente will probably be remembered as the Most Valuable Player of Pittsburgh's 1971 World Series victory, a Series that etched Clemente's greatness into the nation's awareness. He batted .414, hit safely in every game, homered to start the seventh-game victory, was brilliant in the field, and even managed time for some controversy with Baltimore's great Frank Robinson.

When the Series ended, the Pirates victorious, Clemente was called to a microphone in the dressing room. He asked to include a few words in Spanish to his mother and father in Puerto Rico, then said:

"On this, the proudest moment of my life, I ask your blessing."

"Roberto was born to play baseball," his mother, Luisa Walker de Clemente, once said.

"I can remember when he was five years old. He used to buy rubber balls every time he had a chance. He played in his room, throwing the ball against the wall and trying to catch it. There were times when he was so much in love with baseball that he didn't even care for food."

Clemente was born August 18, 1934, the youngest of four sons of a family which lived in the El

Comandante section of Rio Piedras, about ten miles southeast of San Juan. One of his older brothers, Justino, played amateur baseball, and was doing well until he served with the Army in Korea. His mother thought he "never was as good after he left the Army."

Young Roberto kept an album of his baseball feats. One paragraph stood out: "I loved the game so much that even though our playing field was muddy and we had many trees on it, I used to play many hours every day."

An another, describing his batting skills, even at a young age: "The fences were about 150 feet away from home plate and I used to hit many homers. One day I hit 10 home runs in a game we started about 11 A.M. and finished about 6:30 P.M."

In one of his last interviews, Roberto described his childhood: "I was so happy, because my brother and my father and my mother, we used to get together at night, and we used to sit down and make jokes, and we used to eat whatever we had to eat.

"And this is something that was wonderful to me. I grew up with people who really had to struggle to eat. During the war, when food was hard to get, my parents fed their children first and they took what was left. They always thought of us."

Roberto worked as well as played.

He delivered milk for neighbors every day, even though it meant getting up at 6 A.M. before going to school. The large, heavy milk can was awkward to carry, but he stuck with it. And the pay? "They gave me 30 or 31 cents a month," he recalled, "but I said okay."

It took Roberto three years to earn the $27 he needed to buy a second-hand bicycle.

"My father used to say, 'I want you to be a good man, I want you to work, and I want you to be a serious person,'" Clemente said. "I grew up with that in mind."

Maria Isabel Caceres, a history teacher at Julio Vizcarrando High School in Carolina, Puerto Rico, recalled young Roberto as a shy boy who sat in the back of her class and seldom raised his hand or opened his mouth.

"I was astonished to see him on television later speaking so well and without seeming shy because he was very reserved as a child," Mrs. Caceres recalled.

"He was so quiet, so I didn't know him well at first," she said. "But his parents traded at my father's store, so after a while I got to know Roberto better."

Mrs. Caceres gave Clemente a "B" in her history course. It was a good grade considering that the classes were in English and Clemente, at the time, knew little English.

Clemente used to visit his former teacher each year when he went home at the end of the baseball season.

"One time about 1962, he came to the school and they told him my back hurt and I was sick in bed," Mrs. Caceres said. "So he went to my house and I told him how bad I felt and he took me in his arms, right out of bed, and brought me to a doctor. Every day until I could walk, he would bring me over there.

"I asked him once how much it cost, I wanted to pay, and he got mad at me," she said. He told her, "You're offending me by asking."

Each winter Clemente would drop by the school

to say hello to the students. The 1972–73 visit was planned for shortly after New Year's.

In high school, Clemente played on a softball team coached by Mrs. Caceres' husband. "Roberto was a shortstop and he would come to our house to wait for the rest of the players," she said.

"I knew he was good the first time I saw him run. No other athlete like him has ever come out of this school, and we'll probably never have another like him in Puerto Rico," Mrs. Caceres said.

Clemente made the all-star baseball team three years in a row at shortstop. But baseball was not his only sport in high school. He also was the school's "Most Valuable Player" on its track team. He threw the javelin 195 feet. He was a six-foot high jumper. He went 45 feet in the triple jump, then known as the hop, skip and jump. All those figures were outstanding for a high school youth of that era.

The field where Clemente played high school baseball is now part of an enclosed park directly across the street from the school. It long ago was renamed Roberto Clemente Park.

Clemente was considered such a standout in track and field he would probably have qualified for the Puerto Rican team that competed in the 1952 Olympic Games at Helsinki—if he had not signed a professional baseball contract.

It happened this way. When Clemente was an 18-year-old high school kid, he showed up with his torn fielder's glove at a park where the Santurce Crabbers, who played in the Puerto Rican winter league, were working out.

He went on the field with them at shortstop.

Pete Zorrilla, who owned the Santurce team, happened to wander by that day. He noticed Clemente: "You can play for me right now," Zorrilla told the nervous youngster.

The Crabbers offered Clemente $500. And a new glove.

He signed.

"I could see he was going a long way," recalled James Clarkson, the Santurce manager. "Some of the old-timers didn't think so, but I could see great ability in Clemente.

"He had a few rough spots, but he never made the same mistake twice. He had baseball savvy and he listened. He listened to what he was told, and he did it."

Near the end of the 1971 season, Clemente reminisced about his early days in baseball. "The fellow who helped me most of all," he said, "is Buck Clarkson. Buck Clarkson used to tell me I am as good as anybody in big leagues. That helped me a lot."

"The main thing I had to do was to keep his spirits up," Clarkson said. "He didn't realize how good he was.

"But I could see his potential. I had three good outfielders, but I had to give him a chance, and he broke into the regular lineup during the first season I managed Santurce. I always played him in right field and batted him first."

Clarkson also played on the team—at shortstop, which may have been one reason Clemente went on to become a great rightfielder instead of a great shortstop. Managers don't like to bench themselves, even for great young players.

Nevertheless, Clarkson got along well with the young Clemente, although some of the other players resented Roberto. "Some of the old pros didn't take too kindly to a kid breaking into the lineup—but Clemente was too good to keep out," Clarkson said.

That first season at Santurce, Clemente hit .234 with 18 hits in 77 at-bats. (Even after Clemente was signed by a major league club, he continued as a winter league regular for years. In the course of his winter league career, Clemente batted more than 1,900 times—which is the equivalent of four major league seasons.)

"I told him," Buck Clarkson said, "he'd be as good as Willie Mays some day. And he was.

"The big thing about Clemente was that he played hard and went all-out in every game. He did that when he was just a kid, and he did that all the way up through his last season. He always had that aggressiveness. I saw that from the first. Maybe it was the thing about him as a ballplayer that people will remember most."

In the winter of 1953, Al Campanis, a scout for the then Brooklyn Dodgers, chose Clemente from 72 kids at a tryout at Sixto Escobar Stadium. "How could I miss him?" Campanis said. "He was the greatest natural athlete I have ever seen as a free agent."

"The first thing we do at the tryout," Campanis recalled, "is ask the kids to throw from the outfield. This one throws a bullet from center, on the fly. I couldn't believe my eyes.

"Uno mas, I shout, and he does it again. I waved my hand, that's enough. Then we have them run 60 yards. The first time I clock him in 6.4 (seconds). I couldn't believe it. That's in full uniform.

"Uno mas," Campanis shouted again, and again

he did it in 6.4. The other 71 players were sent home.

"The only one I asked to hit was this boy, who told me his name was Roberto Clemente," Campanis said. "He hit for 20, 25 minutes. I'm behind the cage, and I'm saying to myself, we gotta sign this guy if he can just hold the bat in his hands.

"He starts hitting line drives all over the place. I notice the way he's standing in the box, and I figure there's no way he can reach the outside of the plate, so I tell the pitcher to pitch him outside, and the kid swings with both feet off the ground and hits line drives to right and sharp ground balls up the middle."

Needless to say, Campanis was convinced Clemente could hold the bat in his hands.

He said he might have signed Clemente on the spot, but he was still in high school and that was not permissible.

The following spring, however, the Dodgers offered Clemente $10,000. Buck Clarkson urged Clemente to take it. He did not need much urging, even though the Braves, then in Milwaukee, offered $35,000. "I knew most of the fellows who played with the Dodgers, and I was a Dodger fan," Clemente revealed. "Santurce had a working agreement with the Dodgers, which is why I knew most of the fellows there."

The story of Clemente's signing, the year he played for the Dodgers' Montreal farm club in the International League, and his subsequent draft by the Pirates as one of baseball's all-time biggest bargains, is destined to be told as long as baseball is played. It is filled with intrigue.

Buzzi Bavasi, later to run the San Diego Padres,

was the Dodgers' vice president when Clemente was signed. At the time, the major leagues were experimenting with one of several bonus rules they changed yearly in the 1950's. The one in force that year said that any player signed for more than $4,000 had to be placed on the major league roster to be protected from the draft.

If he was not placed on the major league roster, then he would be eligible to be drafted the following season. Since Clemente was paid $10,000 and since he was on the Montreal rather than the Brooklyn roster, he was eligible for the draft.

"You had to be a genius to know he would go on to do what he did," Bavasi said. Be that as it may, the Dodgers had their reasons for assigning Clemente to Montreal instead of Brooklyn. One of them was that the Brooklyn outfield in 1953 consisted of Jackie Robinson in left, Duke Snider in center, and Carl Furillo in right. Robinson hit .329. Snider batted .336 and hit 42 home runs. And Furillo hit .344, best in the league. There was no room in that outfield for a youngster, even if that youngster was named Roberto Clemente.

The Dodgers' main interest was to keep other teams from getting interested in Clemente. More than that, they wanted to be sure that the crosstown Giants would not get hold of him.

"We didn't want the Giants to have Clemente and Willie Mays in the same outfield," Bavasi said. "It was a cheap deal for us."

So the Dodgers tried to "hide" Clemente in Montreal. They kept him on the bench. He played seldom, and when he did get onto the field, funny things happened.

One night the bases were loaded in the first inning when Clemente stepped in to hit. "They called time," Clemente recalled. "Pinch hitter."

There was another night. Although he had hit three triples the night before, Clemente's name was not in the lineup. "They know I'm not used to cold weather," Clemente said. "But when we played in Syracuse, who had the best pitching staff in the league, they'd put me in to pinch-hit. In Richmond, I don't play."

In 1954, Clemente appeared in only 87 games. He came to bat just 148 times. He hit .257 and drove in only 12 runs.

By the end of the season, Clemente was a bewildered and disillusioned youngster, trying to master a strange language in a strange land, and on the verge of going home.

"If they had talked to me, I would never have been so mad," he said. "But it came to where they never told me anything that was going on."

He never could figure out just why the Dodgers thought they could "hide" him. "Everybody knew what I could do," he said. "The Dodgers knew they were going to lose me in the draft, because there were eight teams after me in Puerto Rico. As soon as they put me on the Montreal roster, they knew one of those teams was going to get me."

The Pirates, meanwhile, were in the process of finishing in last place in the National League in 1954, as they generally did in the early 1950's. They knew they would have first choice in the draft.

Their first interest was Joe Black, the standout Dodgers' pitcher who had been sent down to Montreal. Pittsburgh scout Clyde Sukeforth was dispatched to Richmond, where the Montreal team was playing. "I arrived just in time to see the pre-game workouts," he said. "I saw Clemente throwing from the outfield and I couldn't take my eyes off him.

"Later in the game he was used as a pinch hitter and I liked his swing. He impressed me a great deal. I started asking questions and learned he was a bonus player and would be eligible for the draft."

Howie Haak, another Pittsburgh scout, whose thorough scouting in Latin America later helped build the strong Pirates teams of the early 1970's, also was on Clemente's trail. But, he said, "I followed the Montreal club for two weeks and I saw Clemente bat only four times."

"He had so much talent he couldn't hide it," said Bob Fontaine, still another Pirates scout. Clyde Sukeforth again went to watch Montreal. One night he had dinner with Max Macon, the manager. "I don't care if you never play him," Sukeforth told Macon with a grin, "we're going to finish last, and we're going to draft him number one." The Pirates did both those things. They acquired Roberto Clemente for $4,000.

Pittsburgh had a season-opening outfield of Frank Thomas in left field, Earl Smith in center and Roman Mejias in right. Clemente began the 1955 season on the bench, sitting next to Manager Fred Haney.

He made his debut in the fourth game of the season—ironically enough, against the Dodgers. Johnny Podres, a Dodger lefthander, was the opposing pitcher, and Haney put Clemente No. 3 in the batting order. His first time at bat, Clemente beat out an infield single.

Two days later, in his first game in New York,

Clemente hit an inside-the-park homer against the Giants in the Polo Grounds. The pitcher was Don Liddle, another lefthander.

The Pirates lost their first eight games before winning two in a row. Yet Clemente was batting .360. He also was proving to have a temper.

Haney watched wide-eyed as Clemente shattered plastic batting helmets and even bats when he was mad. Haney assessed him a $25 fine after only a month of Clemente's first major league season.

"I don't mind you tearing up your clothes if you want to," Haney told him. "But if you want to destroy club property you're going to have to pay for it."

Another time, Clemente told this story on himself: "Once, I break 22 helmets. Haney, he tells me it will cost me $10 for each one. That's $220, and I do not make so much money. I stop breaking helmets."

Clemente said the lesson taught him to control his temper. In the end, he said, it also helped make him a better ballplayer.

He went on to hit only .255 that first season, although his 121 hits included 39 for extra bases. That year—the year the Dodgers won the pennant, and their very first World Series—Clemente and the Pirates finished last again. It was their fourth successive eighth-place finish.

Besides playing on a losing team, Clemente had some other problems, special problems. He was lonely in Pittsburgh. But he was beginning his warm relationship with the Pirates fans.

"I had no special friends in Pittsburgh," he recalled. "After the games, I was happy to stay behind and sign autographs. I had no place to go. Somehow I feel the 10- and 11-year-old kids of that era became paying customers and were my friends."

His troubles with the English language were only the beginning. But Clemente never lost his sense of humor. In one game at this time, Clemente made a superb catch and robbed the batter of a sure extra base hit. As he trotted toward the dugout at the end of the inning, the batter he had robbed passed him and called him a name that would not normally be considered complimentary.

Clemente, whose English did not include that particular phrase, assumed he was being congratulated. "Sank you," he said politely.

A teammate who overheard the exchange stopped Clemente and said, "What are you thanking him for? Don't you know what he called you?" The teammate then gave Clemente a detailed definition of the three little words directed at him. When Clemente returned to the outfield at the end of the inning, he passed his adversary and returned the compliment not once, not twice, but three times.

In 1956, Clemente suffered the first of the ailments that were to plague him the rest of his life. A back injury incurred in a 1954 automobile accident, began acting up.

"My mother and father wanted me to quit in 1956 and go to school," Clemente said. "My back hurt and I didn't play much in the winter. My people at home, they don't like that. They want me to play, but I say I am hurt.

"I talked to my father and mother and say, I try it one more year. If I still hurt, then I quit. They

21

said okay, but that school would do me good. One winter I did go to school so I can do something good if I can't play baseball."

Despite his physical problems in 1956, Clemente batted .311, third best in the National League. It was the first of what eventually totaled 13 seasons of .300-or-better hitting.

The Pirates also began climbing. In 1956, they managed to finish seventh, only 27 games behind the pennant-winning Dodgers.

When the 1956 season ended, Branch Rickey, then president of the Pirates, made a prediction about Clemente: "In three years, he'll really show you something."

But Clemente's back still was troubling him, and the three years that followed were not three of his best. In 1957, his batting average dipped to .253, lowest of his career. The Pirates and the Chicago Cubs tied for last place in the National League.

In 1958, Clemente's average improved to .289, and the Pirates became a contender. They won 84 games, the most in 20 years. Danny Murtaugh was in his first full year as the Pittsburgh manager. The Pirates finished eight games behind the pennant-winning Braves.

By 1959, Pittsburgh fans began to talk pennant. The All-Star Game was played at Forbes Field, and Vice President Richard M. Nixon came calling. Roberto Clemente batted .296, still improving, but injuries kept him out of a lot of games. He played in only 105. The Pirates skidded to fourth place.

Then came 1960. It was one of the most successful seasons of Clemente's career.

The Pirates started out challenging the defending

champion Dodgers for the pennant. The Dodgers faded. The Braves were still in the race. So were the Cardinals. Down the stretch, everyone had problems.

On Sunday, September 25, 1960, the Pirates played the Braves at Milwaukee. Roberto Clemente had two hits, stole a base and scored a run in the game, and was fourth in the National League batting race at the time. The Pirates lost, 4-2, but it didn't matter. The Braves had already been eliminated. The same day, however, the Cardinals lost 5-0 to the Chicago Cubs, and that loss mattered. It eliminated the Cardinals.

The Pirates were the National League champions for the first time in 33 years. A crowd estimated at 125,000 persons greeted them on their return to Pittsburgh that night.

Clemente finished the season batting .314. He scored 89 runs, had 179 hits, 16 homers, 94 runs batted in. All those marks were highs for the first six years of his career.

People began comparing Clemente to Willie Mays. It was praise, obviously. But to the sensitive Clemente, it was something he did not want to hear. He did not want to be compared to Willie Mays, or to anyone else. He wanted just to be Roberto Clemente, not an imitation of anybody. That was sufficient.

"Many people tell me I wanna play like Willie," Clemente said during the 1960 season. "I no play like Mays. From little boy up, I always play like this," Clemente went on. "I always wanna run fast, to throw long and hit far."

As the Pirates piled up the victories, Clemente received more recognition. He began to think he might deserve the National League's Most Valuable Player Award. It disturbed him that teammate Dick Groat seemed to be politicking for the MVP award with sportswriters. That was something Clemente said he never would do.

Then came the World Series. The Pirates' opponents were the New York Yankees, and everyone expected the Yankees to win easily.

The Pirates won the first game, 6-4. Clemente had one hit and drove in one run. Then Yankee power took over. New York won the second game, 16-3. And the third, 10-0. Clemente had two hits in the second game, one in the third.

Clemente had another hit as Pittsburgh won game four, 3-2, and another in the fifth game, won by the Pirates, 5-2. The Yankees evened the series with a 10-0 victory in the sixth game, despite two hits by Clemente.

Then came the memorable seventh game. The Yankees were ahead 7-4 in the bottom of the eighth, but the Pirates rallied for five runs to go ahead 9-7. They got a big break when a ball hit by Bill Virdon, later to be the Pittsburgh manager, took a bad bounce and struck New York shortstop Tony Kubek on the Adam's apple.

The Yankees tied it in the ninth inning, but Bill Mazeroski homered in the bottom of the ninth. Pittsburgh was the world champion, 10-9.

Along the way, Roberto Clemente got a hit in every game. He was only the 14th player in baseball history to hit safely in every game of a seven-game World Series. He batted .310. It was an occasion that should have been a happy one.

But Clemente did not stay for the locker room

celebration after the final game. Some of Clemente's teammates resented it. "You know where I went?" Clemente said some time later. "I went to Schenley Park to celebrate with the fans. We hugged each other. I felt good being with them." Schenley Park is a large oval park a short distance from Forbes Field, where the Pirates made their home until Three Rivers Stadium was completed in 1970.

A month after the Series, Dick Groat, the 1960 batting champion, was selected as the National League's MVP for 1960. Teammate Don Hoak finished second in the voting by members of the Baseball Writers Association of America. Clemente was not third—or fourth. He was *eighth*. And he was outraged.

"I carried the club all season," Clemente said, feeling he was robbed of the award he deserved. "Sure, Groat had a fine year, but he was injured for a month.

"I had (my) best year in the majors and I was the league's most valuable player, but I didn't get one first place vote.

"I talked to other players in the league and they all told me I was the most valuable," he added.

In mid-season a year later, Clemente still was kicking. He was still insisting he deserved the MVP award, and his argument spread rumors of dissension on the Pirates. "You'll have to take my word for this," said Manager Murtaugh, "but I say there is no dissension on our ball club. I think, meaning morale, the only one who could have been disgruntled was Roberto himself and it hasn't affected his play."

At the time, Clemente was leading the league in hitting.

In the 1961 All-Star Game at San Francisco, Clemente singled to score Willie Mays in the 10th inning and give the National League a 5-4 victory over the American League.

But ironically, the Clemente hit that won the All-Star Game was lost in all the post-game publicity surrounding the fact that gusty winds at Candlestick Park actually blew pitcher Stu Miller off the mound.

Clemente was proud of his game-winning hit, however. Bob Prince, the Pirates' long-time broadcaster, recalled just how proud he was.

"I remember vividly that when he did not win the MVP award in 1960, he would not wear his World Series ring," Prince said. "He felt he had been terribly overlooked and he was very upset about it. He would not wear that ring. He wore instead the All-Star ring because that was the ring that said to him he was the greatest baseball player in the game today."

As things turned out, Dick Groat was traded from the Pirates two years after his 1960 success. In 1968, after his retirement, someone asked him who was the greatest player he ever played with. "I don't know of anybody who played on the same teams with more superstars than I did," said Groat, who was with the Cardinals, Phillies and Giants after he left Pittsburgh. "I was with 'em all, except Hank Aaron and Sandy Koufax, whom I don't count because he was a pitcher. I played with (Stan) Musial with the Cardinals, Clemente with the Pirates,

Richie Allen with the Phillies and Willie Mays with the Giants.

"The best of 'em? For natural tools, I'd have to say Clemente. All around he was the best ballplayer I ever saw."

In 1961, Clemente went on to prove that, at least to a certain extent. He won the first of his four batting titles with a .351 average, which stood as his career high until 1967. He scored 100 runs for the first time, and had 201 hits—the first of four times he exceeded 200. He also had 30 doubles, 10 triples, 23 homers and drove in 89 runs. Included in the average was a remarkable .411 mark for 68 day games.

Clemente was particularly tough on the Chicago Cubs, and some people figured he might have been a .400 hitter for a season someday if he played for the Cubs, who play all their home games in daylight. Baseball has not had a .400 hitter since Ted Williams in 1941 and probably will never have another.

One of Clemente's hits in 1961 was No. 1,000. Just like his first hit, it came at Forbes Field. It was Tuesday night, May 16, 1961, and the Pirates were playing the St. Louis Cardinals. Clemente singled to rightfield off lefthanded pitcher Curt Simmons for the milestone hit. The Pirates won the game, 2-1.

But in 1961, Pittsburgh could not defend its world championship. The Pirates nose-dived all the way to sixth place.

Clemente nevertheless was establishing himself as one of baseball's best hitters. He also was being established as one of its most chronically ill people.

"Sometimes," Clemente confessed during the 1961 season, "I get mad at people. But only once here in

Pittsburgh. That was when I was hurt and everyone call me Jake (baseball slang for a player faking an injury). I don't like that. I want to play but my back hurt lots of times and I can't play.

"You can still feel bone chip in my elbow," he said. "That's why I throw the ball underhand sometimes. That way it doesn't hurt my arm."

Despite his injuries, by the end of the '61 season, Clemente was firmly established as one of baseball's top players.

But before the 1962 season began, he got sick. He had stomach problems. That year his batting average dropped from .351 to .312. The Pirates improved slightly—they finished fourth in the National League, which had expanded to ten teams with the addition of Houston and the New York Mets. That year the Giants won the pennant.

In 1963, the Pirates plummeted all the way to eighth place. Clemente hit .320. He also bumped into trouble—in the form of an umpire. It happened on May 28, 1963, when the Pirates and Phillies were playing a game at Pittsburgh.

Early in the game, first base umpire Bill Jackowski called Pittsburgh's Donn Clendenon out on a close play at first just after the Pirates scored their only run of the game. Murtaugh and Ron Northey, the Pirates' first base coach, argued heatedly with Jackowski. His decision stood.

In the fifth inning, Clemente hit a ground ball with a runner on first base. The Phillies tried for a double play. It was close at first. Jackowski signalled "out."

Clemente was incensed. He was certain he was safe.

He started toward Jackowski. Northey stepped

28

between them. Clemente tried to brush past the coach. His hand struck the umpire.

Jackowski ejected Clemente from the game and reported the incident to the National League office. Warren Giles, the league president, made the decision. Clemente, he said, was fined $250 and suspended for five days.

Now, Clemente was really furious.

"This was an accident," he insisted. "I hit him with my open palm, not my fist, but this was because I was trying to get away from the coach."

Clemente pointed out that Leo Durocher had been given only a three-day suspension two seasons earlier when he kicked umpire Jocko Conlan in the shins. "What I did was mild compared to what Durocher did to Conlan," Clemente complained.

But Giles said Clemente's actions "were the most serious reported to our office in several years."

"How can Giles say this?" Clemente demanded, "when Durocher did what he did? I had good reason for losing my head. Durocher didn't."

Clemente was so outraged that he even sat down and wrote a letter to Giles. Giles answered: "Even though you may be very angry, you must try to control your temper in the presence of umpires."

Giles never did say why Durocher's suspension had been only for three days, but the reason may have been that when Durocher kicked Conlan, Conlan kicked him back.

The incident helped establish Clemente as a leader on the Pirates club. He spoke out about umpiring in general in the league. "Every year," he charged, "I lose 15 or 20 points on close plays at first base. This is the worst year for umpiring.

"Other teams argue and get close decisions," he

added. "Dodgers get every close play. Why? We don't argue and we don't get them.

"I seldom argue unless I feel umpire is wrong," Clemente went on, and then came the kicker: There were, he said, "only two or three good umpires" in the National League.

Ever since he reached the major leagues in 1955, Clemente had argued with umpires. "This was because I was trying to win a job," he explained, "and I figure that when an umpire gives me a bad call, he is keeping me from this job."

But by the mid-1960's Clemente began to figure that neither umpires nor pitchers could be much of a deterrent to a man with his skills. Advice he received from an unexpected source convinced him it was necessary to play the game with a cooler head.

One of Clemente's brothers was dying of cancer. It was nothing so dramatic as a death-bed lecture, but it still made a large impression on Clemente. "He tell me," Clemente recalled years later, "to quit fighting the umpires. He say to me: 'You are too good a ballplayer to worry about them. Just go and play your game.'"

In the later years of his career, Clemente was milder toward umpires. In fact, in 1970, Clemente served as the peacemaker in a fight between the Pirates and Cubs in Chicago and was commended by the umpires for his effort.

Clemente came to enjoy banter with umpires during dead spots on the field. Once in a game at San Diego, when he was hitting only about .225—it was still early in the season—Clemente was thrown out of a game by umpire Lee Weyer.

"The way you're goin', you'd be better off out of the game anyway," Weyer told him.

"When he said that," Clemente remarked later, "there was not anything left for me to say."

In 1964, Clemente won his second batting title. He hit .339, had 211 hits (a career high), 40 doubles (another career high), and drove in 87 runs. The Pirates and Dodgers tied for sixth place.

Clemente was starting to earn big money in baseball, although he still was a couple of years away from the $100,000 plateau. But on occasion he still had to fight prejudices.

He used to tell the story of an expedition with his wife to buy furniture in New York City. Later, he was to become a hero to New York's Puerto Rican community, and 44,000 people came out to a routine game at Shea Stadium to honor him, but the furniture people apparently never had heard of him.

"The people met us at the door and said, 'What do you want?' " Clemente recounted. "We said we would like to see the showroom and see some furniture.

"They told us to wait a little bit, they were going to send somebody to the last floor to see what they they have. So they said they had one floor of furniture, and they took us there to see it.

"But that furniture they were showing us upstairs wasn't what they had in the showroom. I told them we would like to see the furniture downstairs, that was in the showroom.

"They said, 'Well, you don't have enough money to buy that.' and I said, 'How do you know that I don't have enough money?' and they said, 'That's very expensive.'

"I said, 'Well, I would like to see it, because I have the right to see it. I have the right to it as a human being, as a person who comes to buy from you.' So finally they showed it to us."

Clemente, who with his wife was preparing for a trip to Europe at the time, had $5,000 in his wallet. "I took the whole amount of money and said, 'Do you think this much can buy it?'

"So now they wanted to know who I was and all this stuff, and when they found out who I was, they said they have seven floors full of furniture, and don't worry about it, they're going to show it to me. They said, 'We thought you were, like, another Puerto Rican.' And right away, I just got mad. I said, 'Look, your business is to sell to anybody, I don't care if I'm Puerto Rican or if I'm Jewish or whatever you want to call me.'

"This is what really gets me mad. Because I'm Puerto Rican, they treat me different." Clemente stuffed the five grand back into his wallet and walked out of the store.

In 1964, Clemente began to complain of insomnia. He said the snoring of roommate Gene Baker kept him awake at night. In 1965, when the Pirates traveled, Clemente had a private room.

But the biggest difference between 1964 and 1965 was that Danny Murtaugh stepped down as manager because of problems with his health, and Harry Walker replaced him.

Clemente and Murtaugh had not gotten along well during that part of their careers. Clemente suspected, with good reason, that Murtaugh did not believe him when Clemente said he was ill.

One of his reasons was an incident in 1963. Clemente contracted food poisoning in Los Angeles and, feeling weak, did not play well against the Dodgers.

A couple of days later, the team was in Houston. Clemente still felt ill—and said so.

Murtaugh called him to the manager's office and told him, as Clemente somewhat sarcastically remembered it, that he was going to get a rest. "You let me know when you are ready to play again," Clemente said Murtaugh told him. "You're making too much money to sit on the bench. The next time you feel like playing you'll play and you'll play every day until I say you won't play."

"You talk like I don't want to play baseball," Clemente replied.

"I don't care what you think, and that's all I'm going to say," Clemente said Murtaugh told him.

There was another incident in Philadelphia. Clemente was playing with two stitches in his ankle, and had trouble running. He hit a drive to shortstop and fell coming out of the batter's box. The Phillies were throwing the ball around the infield by the time he got up.

Clemente came back to the bench and told Murtaugh he could not play. Murtaugh disagreed, and said, "If you don't get in there, it'll cost you a hundred and fifty."

"I'm not playing," Clemente persisted.

"Then make it two-fifty," Murtaugh said. "I'm still not playing," Clemente said.

"It's three-fifty," Murtaugh replied. The conversation did not end until the fine reached $650. Clemente stayed on the bench and paid the fine.

Once, Clemente told writers, "Danny Murtaugh

can kiss my nasty foot," or something like that, perhaps a little more graphically.

"Murtaugh had no respect for me, and I had no respect for him," Clemente said.

Clemente claimed that his image as baseball's most publicized hypochondriac was Murtaugh's fault. He became one of the game's top players when Murtaugh was the Pittsburgh manager, but Clemente said this was in spite of Murtaugh, and not because of him.

"Nobody had better years under Murtaugh than me," he said. "But he acted like he didn't appreciate me. Instead of being friendly, he needled me."

Things were to be very different later, but that was how Clemente felt about Murtaugh in 1965. He was still having problems convincing people that he was ill when he said he was. One reason was the simple fact that he was a better player sick than most people are when they are healthy. Such problems nearly sent his relationship with Harry Walker, the new Pittsburgh manager, onto the rocks.

In January, 1965, Clemente underwent an operation to remove a blood clot from his right thigh. In February he came down with a virus, which was diagnosed as malaria in March.

The Pirates got off to a bad start under their new manager, and Clemente, not fully recovered from his illnesses, was playing poorly. Before the season was a month old, Clemente stormed into the Pirates' clubhouse at Wrigley Field in Chicago and announced, "I want to be traded from this club and I don't want to play for this manager (Walker) any more."

A day later, however, Clemente and Walker huddled over breakfast. Clemente later appeared and said his outburst was "misunderstood."

"You just blow off steam when you can't play (well)," said Clemente. "I don't want to be traded. I want to play—but not bad ball."

After their meeting, Walker said, "Clemente said he liked me and appreciated my problems.

"He felt since he was getting the brunt of the blame, he figured maybe a trade would solve things," Walker said, "but I believe we understand each other now."

Their relationship did indeed become a good one. Within a year, Clemente could say, "Harry Walker is the best manager I've ever had."

Walker said that before he became manager of the Pirates he had "heard rumors that Clemente was hard to get along with."

"Yes, we had that one little misunderstanding (in Chicago)," Walker said, "but from that point on we communicated with each other and believed in each other. I've never lied to him. I always tried to be fair and I think that means a lot to someone as high-spirited as Clemente."

In 1965, Clemente batted .329, and won his third National League batting title. The Pirates got back into contention, finishing in third place, seven games behind the Los Angeles Dodgers.

But 1965 was eventful for other reasons for Clemente, too. For the first of two times in his career, he said he did not want to play in the All-Star Game. He said he preferred to rest during the three-day All-Star break, but the real reason was probably his pride. He had not been voted to the starting lineup, but was added to the team as a substitute by All-Star manager, Gene Mauch of the Phillies.

Mauch then called Clemente on the telephone, and assuaged his wounded pride. "It wouldn't be an All-Star team without Clemente," Mauch said.

Clemente played.

Clemente did not want to play again in the 1970 All-Star Game, claiming he needed the time off for a sore neck. "The hell with the All-Star Game," he said.

Again, he had not been voted to the squad, but had been picked for backup by Gil Hodges of the Mets, the NL manager that year. Hodges refused to do as Mauch had done and call Clemente. "I will not do it," Hodges said. "I won't call him. This is Roberto Clemente's decision and nobody else's."

A day later, Clemente said he had changed his mind. He played in the game.

Two years later, Clemente got up in front of a microphone in Atlanta the night before the All-Star Game and said:

"The players who say they don't want to play in an All-Star Game and would rather sit home and rest are not telling the truth. What they say that comes out of their mouth and what they say that goes into their mouth is not the same thing."

The irony of that is that in 1972, Clemente did not play in the game. He suffered a badly bruised left knee in the last regular game before the All-Star Game and still was limping noticeably the night of the game. Willie Mays replaced him in the starting lineup.

But back to 1966. How was Clemente's season?

He batted .317. He had a career high 119 RBIs, a career high 29 homers, 31 doubles, 11 triples, scored a career high 105 runs and had 202 hits.

On September 2nd, he drove a fastball from Ferguson Jenkins of the Cubs into the upper deck in right field at Forbes Field. The home run was Clemente's 2,000th major league hit.

His leadership and his hitting kept the Pirates in the pennant race until the final weekend. But on a dreary Saturday at Forbes Field, the next-to-last day of the season, Pittsburgh lost a doubleheader to the San Francisco Giants and was eliminated. The Dodgers won the pennant on the final day. San Francisco was second. Pittsburgh finished third.

But Clemente finished first. In November, the announcement came from the Baseball Writers Association. Clemente had beaten out Sandy Koufax for the Most Valuable Player award in the National League.

"This is the first year a manager made me feel like I wanted to keep going all the time," Clemente said when it was over. "He (Walker) did the job. Maybe he isn't the best manager in the game, but he works hard."

"I knew when I first joined this club," Harry Walker said, "that the one thing Clemente wanted most in life was to be the MVP."

"I think he was the MVP because he did so many little things, things that some stars don't do, hustling on routine ground balls, breaking up double plays, and hustling to take an extra base," Harry Walker said. "By doing this, he set an example that the others followed and this made him the Most Valuable Player."

"This is the new Clemente," added teammate Donn Clendenon. "I always thought the guy had great ability, but until the last two years (1965 and 1966), I thought he was playing for himself. But in the last two years, he developed into the leader of our ballclub."

This also was the season that Clemente began speaking out against the lack of status accorded Latin ballplayers. "The Latin American player doesn't get the recognition he deserves," Clemente said. "Neither does the Negro player, unless he does something really spectacular, like Willie Mays.

"We have self-satisfaction, yes. But after the season is over, nobody cares about us. Zoilo Versalles (Minnesota Twins) was the Most Valuable Player in the American League (1965), but how many times has he been asked to make appearances at dinners or meetings during the winter?" Clemente said.

"Juan Marichal is one of the greatest pitchers in the game, but does he get invited to banquets?

"Somebody says we live too far away. That's a lousy excuse. I am an American citizen. But some people act like they think I live in the jungle some place. To the people, we are outsiders, foreigners."

The winter of 1966-67 was one of great content for Clemente. In Puerto Rico, Clemente opened a new restaurant and bar near San Juan.

The Pirates made a trade with the Los Angeles Dodgers, acquiring infielder Maury Wills, and Clemente—among others—predicted that the move would bring the 1967 pennant to Pittsburgh.

Wills, a cunning veteran who played in four World Series with the Dodgers, did his part in 1967. He batted .302. Clemente did his part too.

On May 15, 1967, Clemente had perhaps the finest game of his career as a hitter, at least up to that time. The Pirates were playing the Cincinnati Reds at Crosley Field in Cincinnati. In the first inning, with Wills on base, Clemente hit a home run against pitcher Milt Pappas. He came up in the fifth with Wills on base again, and hit another homer off Pappas. In the eighth, Clemente slammed a two-run double. And in the ninth, facing pitcher Gerry Arrigo with the bases empty, Clemente homered again.

He had hit three home runs and a double and driven in seven runs. But the Reds also had seven. In the 10th inning, Cincinnati won, 8-7. "I would rather win," Clemente said, his own heroics forgotten.

A couple of weeks later, the Pirates were still not winning. Clemente—by now, an acknowledged leader of the team—called all the players together for a pre-game meeting. The coaches and the manager were not permitted to attend.

"I know there are some players who don't like Walker and don't like me," Clemente said. "Walker is our manager and we must do what he tells us, whether we like him or not.

"If you have any gripes about the manager, about me, or anybody else, now speak up. We can settle it here." Clemente said nothing much was settled.

In mid-June, the club still was going bad. Walker had been giving Clemente an occasional rest, but Clemente apparently felt he had to do more to take charge. So he told Walker he wanted to play every game "until I drop dead."

But still the Pirates did not win. Many players who had exceptional seasons in the 1966 pennant race simply fell apart in '67.

In mid-season, General Manager Brown called together all the writers covering the team for an informal press conference at Forbes Field. The rumors were out that Walker's job as manager was in jeopardy, and Brown wanted to let everyone know that was not true. "Harry Walker will be the Pirates' manager for a long time to come," Brown said.

A "long time" turned out to be two weeks. Walker was fired in mid-July.

The management named an interim manager of the club, to finish the 1967 season. He was Danny Murtaugh.

Someone asked Clemente's opinion. "I play for any manager," he said. And Murtaugh responded that he did not think he would have any trouble getting along with anyone hitting as well as Clemente was hitting. They did get along. Clemente finished the season with a .357 batting average, best of his career, had a career-high 209 hits, drove in 110 runs, and won his fourth—and last—batting championship.

But rather than fuss with Murtaugh anymore, Clemente got into it with his teammates for a change. "There are a few players on this team," he said, "who can be blamed for our poor showing. They know who they are." Clemente refused to name names, but he said the Pirates should not "be where we are today."

His teammates resented the charge that some of them were slacking off. "If you're going to make such charges, it's only fair to the rest of the team to name names," said one. "The way it is now, all the fans are guessing which players Clemente is talking about. And we're all under a cloud of sorts."

Another said, "He's always complaining about being exhausted. He doesn't seem to think any of the rest of us get tired."

Pittsburgh finished in sixth place. The Pirates had a new manager in 1968, Larry Shepard, who had spent almost his entire career managing in the minor leagues.

Shepard had one idea that never went over too well with Clemente. He believed the Pirates should trade Clemente and get a few younger players for him. Naturally, it was not an idea destined to bring Clemente and Shepard close.

Clemente had other problems. Over the winter, he was injured in an accident at home. "I'm lucky to be alive," he said. "I have these iron bars on the back of my house. I called to my wife, Vera, that I was going to lift myself up to the back porch. Just as she came out the back door, I grabbed the iron bar and it gave way.

"It almost fell on my chest. It could have crushed me. I fell backwards, and somehow pushed the bar off, and I began to roll down the hill behind my house. I must have rolled 75 or 100 feet. I went over on my shoulder several times, but the bar didn't hit me." The bar, Clemente said, was about three inches in diameter and four feet long.

The shoulder bothered him all season. In May, Clemente was hitting .211. He rallied to finish at .291 after batting .300-or-better for eight straight years.

The Pirates finished sixth again. Clemente was disappointed by the season. He talked, at age 34, of retiring. His doctor came from Puerto Rico to Pittsburgh to examine the shoulder. But he gave no assurance it would heal over the winter.

Clemente did not retire, however. He came back swinging—first, at his critics. The Pirates were in Miami near the end of March, 1969, in spring training, when Clemente accused sportswriters of trying to ruin his image "because I am black and Puerto Rican."

It had been written that Clemente was not a team player, and he wanted to set the record straight.

"I win four batting titles," he bellowed. "I kill myself in outfield. I try to catch everything in the ball park. I play when I hurt. What more do you writers want from me?"

Clemente then spat into his glove. He rubbed the saliva round the pocket, scowling all the while.

"Did any ballplayer ever come up to you and say I no team player? Who say that? The writers, right? Well, I tell you one thing, the more I can stay away from the writers the better I am. You know why? Because they are trying to create a bad image for me.

"You know what they have against me? Because I am black and Puerto Rican. I am proud to be Puerto Rican."

But a couple of days later, Clemente tempered his remarks and said, "I respect some sportswriters.

"If you come to me and say, 'Roberto, I think you made a bad play,' I don't get mad. I feel you are being honest. I may not agree with you, but you are being honest," he said. "What burns me is when somebody says: 'Somebody said . . .' Then I challenge them and they can't tell me who 'somebody' is."

The Pittsburgh fans apparently took umbrage.

Clemente got off to a bad start in 1969. Then it finally happened. Clemente was booed in Pittsburgh.

On April 12, the Pirates were playing the Phillies. Clemente hit into a bases-loaded double play to kill a Pittsburgh rally.

The next day, he hit into another double play in the fourth inning. When he came to bat in the sixth ining, he was booed by the fans. It was the first time in 15 seasons.

He hit into another double play. Then he committed a two-base error in right field in the top of the eighth.

In the bottom of the eighth inning, Clemente came up again to hit. Again he was booed. But Clemente, ever the showman, refused to let it disturb him. The Pirates fans always had been good to him, and he would not let one brief moment spoil 15 good years. So he encouraged them. He gave the booing crowd a frivolous wave of his batting helmet.

And you know what happened?

About half the boos suddenly became applause.

Then Clemente, despite continuing problems with his shoulder and his sleep and a torn thigh muscle, went out and played the rest of the year like a man with something to prove.

In August, he was having problems finding the right bat to use. He used five different bats in a game at San Francisco on August 13, but, he said, "I do that a lot." In that game Clemente hit three home runs for the second time in his career, doing it on his first three at-bats in the first, third and sixth innings.

He was one swing away from joining the select group of major leaguers who hit four homers in a single game.

In the eighth inning, Clemente singled. But he had one more chance. He came to bat in the ninth, still looking for No. 4. But he grounded out instead.

The Pirates won the game, 10-5.

Roberto Clemente was five days short of his 35th birthday. He was challenging for a fifth batting title.

In September, the pennant already was gone. The National League had expanded to 12 teams and split into two divisions and the miracle Mets were battling the Cubs for the lead.

It also seemed that the batting title was gone. With a week left in the season, the Mets' Cleon Jones led the batting race with a .346 average. Pete Rose of Cincinnati was at .344. Clemente was hitting .335.

Then Clemente got three hits in a doubleheader against Philadelphia. The Pirates played the Cubs in a weekend series, and Clemente had two hits in each game. He had gone 9-for-17 and moved past the slumping Jones into second place behind Rose.

The batting championship was still in sight as the Pirates went up against the Montreal Expos in the final two games of the year.

On October 1, Clemente got two hits against Montreal and edged closer to Rose.

Then came the final game of the year. Clemente knew he would need a miracle finish to win it. He got three straight hits.

In Atlanta, where the Cincinnati Reds were finishing their season, Rose was hitless. One more hit and Clemente could win the title.

Clemente went up at bat. He made an out.

Now it was up to Rose. On his final at-bat of the season, Pete bunted for a single. He won the batting championship with a .348 average. Clemente was second at .345, despite a brilliant finish that saw him bat .538 in the final seven games.

But now it was time for the Pirates to look to 1970. Larry Shepard, unable to produce a champion in two seasons, was fired. The new Pittsburgh manager was an old one. Danny Murtaugh, given a clean bill of health by his doctors, returned.

Inevitably, the writers predicted trouble between Murtaugh and Clemente.

But Clemente was going to be 36 years old in 1970. He was acknowledged as the team's leader. Murtaugh also showed signs that he was a different man than in his first stint as manager. He seemed to realize that Clemente did need an occasional rest, that he was a man playing with injuries. And under Murtaugh's astute leadership, Clemente was to enjoy two of his finest years in 1970 and 1971.

At the end of the '71 season, Clemente was to observe of his former antagonist:

"I would say that Murtaugh used me pretty good the last two years. He gave me lots of rest."

It did not begin that way. Clemente was talking retirement when he reported to spring training in 1970.

"The money," he said, "isn't everything. If I have enough to provide for my family and my relatives in Puerto Rico, then I will be satisfied. This could be my last year."

Clemente also had an idea to conserve his energy. "I don't want to make any trips during spring training," he said.

"If Danny Murtaugh wants him to make the trips, he will," Brown said.

Clemente made the trips.

Once the season began, the Pirates started winning. Clemente was challenging for another batting title. Everyone in Pittsburgh was happy.

In July, the Pirates moved out of Forbes Field. Their new stadium, Three Rivers Stadium, was opened. A writer asked Clemente if he regretted leaving Forbes Field, where he began his career and rose to fame.

"Well, I guess you can say it's like being married 16 years to the same woman and then moving on to another wife," he wisecracked.

The Pirates were in their new park barely a week when they finally paid homage to Roberto Clemente. On "Roberto Clemente Night," July 24, 1970, 43,290 people came out to see Clemente get two hits in three at-bats as the Pirates walloped the Houston Astros 11-0. Many in the crowd had come from Puerto Rico.

Later that night, after things had quieted down, someone asked Roberto Clemente what that night had meant to him.

"In a moment like this," he said, "you can see a lot of years in a few minutes. You can see everything firm and you can see everything clear.

"I don't know if I cried, but I am not ashamed to cry. I would say a man never cries from pain or from disappointment, but if you know the history of our island, the way we were brought up, you ought to remember we're a sentimental people.

"I don't have the word to say how I feel when I step on that field and know that so many are behind me, and know that so many represent my island and Latin America."

In August, a bizarre tale was revealed of a happening a year earlier in San Diego. A reporter found out that Clemente had been kidnapped at gunpoint during a 1969 trip by the Pirates, driven to an isolated mountain, and ordered to strip.

The abductors took his wallet, All-Star game ring and about $250 cash he had in his wallet. "This is when I figure they are going to shoot me and throw me into the woods," Clemente said. "They already have the pistol inside my mouth."

Clemente began to talk. He told them he was a ballplayer. He told them to check his wallet for a membership card in the Baseball Players' Association. "And my ring," he said. "My All-Star ring. That is proof."

One of the men, apparently a Mexican, spoke Spanish. Clemente believed that helped his chances. He was given his clothes, money, wallet and ring, and driven back to his hotel.

Some people, particularly ballplayers, thought the story too kooky to be true. But no one could figure out why Clemente would make it up.

Two weeks later, when the Pirates were playing on the West Coast, a San Diego police detective verified Clemente's account of the incident.

Meanwhile, Roberto was concerned with more immediate things.

On August 22, he went 5-for-7 in a 16-inning, 2-1 victory for the Pirates over the Dodgers at Los Angeles. The next day he got five more hits, in six at-bats, as Pittsburgh beat Los Angeles 11-0. It was the first time in modern major league history—the first time since 1900—a player had made 10 hits in two successive games.

Clemente was hitting .363 and again leading the race for a fifth batting title.

But then he had another problem.

On September 4, Clemente felt a twinge in his back as he was batting in the first inning of a game with the Phillies at Three Rivers Stadium in Pittsburgh. It turned out to be a sprained muscle.

Clemente would play very little the final month of the season. His average dropped from .358 to .352. Rico Carty of Atlanta won the batting title.

The Pirates, however, held on. They won the National League's Eastern Division title.

In the championship playoffs against the Reds, Clemente was not up to par. The Pirates never got a batting attack going. They were defeated in three successive low-scoring games.

That winter, Clemente decided to try his hand at managing. "If a black player wants to become a manager, the owners tell him he has to go to the minors to get experience," Clemente said. "But a white player does not. And sometimes the white player has not even made it to the major leagues.

"I think that is a double standard."

But Clemente said he was not interested in getting a major league managing job for himself—although he would try it in the winter league to see how he liked it.

Clemente quickly found out that he had a bad problem. Manager Clemente did not have a player like Clemente on the roster. He found it frustrating.

He also found trouble—a run-in with a player. Mike Cuellar, a pitcher who won 24 games for the world champion Baltimore Orioles in 1970, quit Clemente's San Juan team. "I'm disgusted," Cuellar said, after Clemente yanked him in the third inning of a game.

"I tell him he's not pitching the way we want him to pitch," Manager Clemente said. "I tell him his arm is not in shape, and when it is, he can pitch for me again."

Cuellar said only, "I'm in no condition to pitch the way Clemente wants me to."

They did not know it at the time, but there was going to be another confrontation the following year.

In 1971, everyone was talking about the "Big Red Machine," the Cincinnati team that had beaten the Pirates for the National League championship in 1970. But people in Pittsburgh thought their club was ready. The Pirates had had an infusion of youth in the late 1960's. Players like Al Oliver and Bob Robertson and Richie Hebner and Manny Sanguillen were starting to become solid major league regulars.

Pittsburgh was favored to win the East again and Cincinnati was expected to win in the West. But the "Big Red Machine" collapsed. The Pirates did not.

With Dock Ellis, a controversial young pitcher, getting off to a brilliant start, and Willie Stargell hitting home runs almost daily for a while, the Pirates opened a big lead in the Eastern Division.

Ellis earned the starting job for the National League in the All-Star game and eventually finished with 19 victories despite late-season elbow trouble. Stargell hit 48 home runs, most in the major leagues. And while Roberto Clemente hit a most productive .341, he was not the key factor in the pennant race.

The Pirates won the East by seven games. They

played the San Francisco Giants, surprise winners of the West, in the best-of-5 playoffs. The Giants won the first game, 5-4. In the second game at Candlestick Park, Clemente had three hits. But the story of the game was Robertson's three homers. Pittsburgh won 9-4 to even the series. In the third, Hebner hit a homer to give Pittsburgh a 2-1 victory.

In game four, Clemente had two hits and drove in three runs. His run-scoring single put the Pirates ahead to stay. They won 9-5.

Pittsburgh was the National League champion for 1971, and the stage was set for Clemente's biggest moment.

The statement may be disputed by some, but most knowledgeable observers consider the World Series to be the nation's No. 1 sports spectacle. The Super Bowl comes and goes in a day, but the World Series builds in excitement from one game through as many as seven. When a World Series goes the seven-game limit, there is nothing to compare with the excitement of that seventh game. This one was to go seven—although hardly anyone thought so at the start.

The Baltimore Orioles again were the American League champions. They were in the World Series on the strength of brilliant pitching, boasting four 20-game winners. The Pirates had not had a 20-game winner in 11 years. Almost everyone figured the Orioles would win easily, and that was the way it started.

Baltimore won the first two games at Baltimore, 5-3 and 11-3. Then they headed for Pittsburgh to finish the job. Roberto Clemente had a prediction. "When we get to Pittsburgh," he said, "things will be a little different. "

Clemente said the field in Baltimore was not up to major league standards. "This is the worst field I've ever played on," he complained.

Frank Robinson, who plays right field for the Orioles, told Clemente he ought to stop worrying about the field and start worrying about his ballclub. In so many words, Robinson told Clemente to quit being a crybaby.

But the Series had a long way to go.

The Pirates won the third game, 5-1, and the fourth, 4-3. Clemente had three hits in the fourth game. He was routinely brilliant throughout the Series. The Pirates had not yet won it, but Dick Young of the New York *Daily News,* one of the nation's most respected baseball writers, wrote: "The best damn ballplayer in the World Series, maybe in the whole world, is Roberto Clemente, and as far as I'm concerned they can give him the automobile (which goes to the Series MVP) right now.

"Maybe some guys hit the ball farther, and some throw it harder, and one or two run faster, although I doubt that, but nobody puts it all together like Roberto."

Thursday, October 14, was a clear, bright day in Pittsburgh. Nelson Briles pitched a magnificent, two-hit shutout, and the Pirates beat the Orioles, 4-0. They were going back to Baltimore—and they were going back with the lead.

The Orioles won the sixth game on Saturday. They won it because they found the Pittsburgh weakness. "Clemente is good," Frank Robinson remarked later—"but even Clemente can only play one position at a time."

Clemente had made a great throw from right field in the ninth inning to prevent the Orioles from scoring the winning run. But in the 10th, Frank Robinson took some liberties on the arm of centerfielder Vic Davalillo and raced home with the run that gave Baltimore a 3-2 victory.

There was going to be a seventh game.

Mike Cuellar, the Baltimore ace, the man the Orioles turn to in key situations, was on the mound for the final game. The same Mike Cuellar who had quit Clemente's San Juan team the previous winter.

It was a cool and cloudy day in Baltimore, but somehow the seventh game of a World Series provides its own heat. There was electricity in the air.

Cuellar retired the first 11 Pittsburgh batters in order, permitting only two balls to be hit beyond the infield. The game was scoreless until the fourth inning.

Then with two out in the top of the fourth inning, Clemente drove a high curve ball from Cuellar over the centerfield fence for a home run. Pittsburgh led, 1-0.

The score remained 1-0 until the eighth, when the Pirates got another run. Baltimore also got one but Pittsburgh won, 2-1. The Pirates were the world champions.

When it came time to vote for the Most Valuable Player award, it was almost automatic.

Roberto Clemente had dominated the Series with his hitting, his fielding, his running. He had 12 hits, including two homers, two doubles and a triple. He batted .414. For the second time he had hit safely in all games of a seven-game World Series. He was the MVP, and he same to New York to receive his convertible.

"Now," said Clemente, cracking one of his infrequent smiles, "everyone knows the way Roberto Clemente plays. I believe I'm the best player in baseball today . . . and I'm glad I was able to show it against Baltimore in the Series."

There was really only one goal left for Clemente as a baseball player—to join the 10 other greats who had achieved 3,000 hits. He needed only 118 more. But for a time he thought of foregoing that prize.

Before the seventh game of the World Series, Clemente had told Howie Haak, "If we win today, I'm announcing my retirement after the game."

Everybody likes to go out on top. But one thing changed Clemente's mind. "When I came off the field, I saw my wife standing near the dugout," he said. "She was crying. Crying for happiness.

"When I spoke with her, she told me she didn't want me to do it. That's all. So I said all right, I'm gonna try to keep playing a few more years."

In the off-season Clemente turned to other interests, including his dream to build a "Sports City" complex for Puerto Rican youth. "I like working with kids," Clemente said. "I don't charge anything for it, I put my money into it."

Clemente planned the facility as one that could use the best coaches available to give youngsters a chance to develop whatever talents they have. "Lots of kids don't participate in sports because they don't like one particular sport," Clemente said. "But if you have all sports where they can participate, I bet you that kids will like at least one of them and keep going with that."

In Houston, where he received one of the many awards that accrued to him, Clemente explained his philosophy of helping young people. "Any time you have the opportunity to accomplish something for somebody who comes behind you and you don't do it, you are wasting your time on this earth," he said.

In the spring of 1972, Clemente told me that 1972 or 1973 would be his final season in the majors. "There is no way I will play after 1973," he said.

In the meantime, he set out in quest of his 3,000th hit. Only 10 players in history ever had made that many hits. Only two of them, Willie Mays and Hank Aaron, were still playing.

By mid-summer, he had just about given up hope of getting No. 3,000 in 1972. Ankle and heel injuries kept him out of 47 of Pittsburgh's first 116 games, and he was used only as a pinch hitter in five others.

In August, he began to feel better. He was closing in on the mark. In September, playing in daylight at Chicago's Wrigley Field, where he always hit well, he was super.

Clemente went into Wrigley Field needing 22 more hits to reach 3,000. He got eight in three games. The Pirates won all three. They led the Eastern Division by 15 games. The pennant race was a joke—the race was for No. 3,000.

On September 27, Clemente got two hits at Philadelphia. Two to go.

The next night, he got No. 2,999. Then he pulled himself out of the game. The Pirates were going home September 29 for a weekend series with the Mets, and Clemente wanted to get No. 3,000 at Three Rivers Stadium.

Friday night, September 29, 1972, a crowd of

24,193 turned out on a soggy night in Pittsburgh to see the Pirates play the Mets. Tom Seaver was the New York pitcher.

On Clemente's first at-bat in the bottom of the first inning, he hit a bouncer over the pitcher's mound toward second baseman Ken Boswell.

Boswell appeared to have a good chance to get Clemente at first. But he bobbled the ball and Clemente was safe.

The official scorer, Luke Quay of the *McKeesport Daily News,* announced in the press box, "Error second baseman . . . error Boswell."

But the people working one deck above on the electric scoreboard apparently could not hear the call. Nothing was posted on the scoreboard. The fans began to cheer. Ed Kranepool, the New York first baseman, retrieved the ball and flipped it to Clemente, who held it for a moment.

Then the error was posted. There were some boos. Clemente was not to get a hit that night.

Afterward, he was mad. "All my life," he complained, "they have been stealing hits from me. They have done this to me all the time. Just because I speak my mind and tell them what I think of them they give me the shaft and take many hits away from me."

A writer protested: "You have many friends in the press box, Roberto. They call them the way they see them."

"Sure, I have friends," Clemente answered. "I have writers who stay at my house in Puerto Rico. There is the other kind, too, who don't like me because I say what I think to them. That's why they give me the works."

But in true Clemente fashion, he calmed down after a couple of minutes. "Deep down, I think I would rather have a clean hit," he said.

The next day, September 30, he got it.

At 3:07 P.M. on a Saturday afternoon in Pittsburgh, Mets pitcher Jon Matlack—later named the National League's rookie-of-the-year in 1972—threw Clemente a curve ball. Clemente hit it into the gap in left center field for a fourth inning double.

It was his 3,000th hit. It also was to be his last in regular-season play.

Clemente rested until the playoffs began. The Pirates coasted to the N.L. East title, but they had their problems with the Cincinnati Reds, who won in the West. It figured to be a close play-off, and it was.

Clemente made only four hits in 17 at-bats in five games, a .235 average. The teams went to the final half-inning of the final game, and the Reds won the pennant when the winning run scored on a wild pitch with two outs. Clemente would not be playing in the World Series in 1972.

Or ever again.

Clemente's record

WITH PITTSBURGH

Regular Season

Year	G	AB	R	H	HR	RBI	Avg.
1955	124	474	48	121	5	47	.255
1956	147	543	66	169	7	60	.311
1957	111	451	42	114	4	30	.253
1958	140	519	69	150	6	50	.289
1959	105	432	60	128	4	50	.296
1960	144	570	89	179	16	94	.314
1961	146	572	100	201	23	89	.351
1962	144	538	95	168	10	74	.312
1963	152	600	77	192	17	76	.320
1964	155	622	95	211	12	87	.339
1965	152	589	91	194	10	65	.329
1966	154	638	105	202	29	119	.317
1967	147	585	103	209	23	110	.357
1968	132	502	74	146	18	57	.291
1969	138	507	87	175	19	91	.345
1970	108	412	65	145	14	60	.352
1971	132	522	82	178	13	86	.341
1972	102	378	68	118	10	60	.312
TOTAL	2,433	9,454	1,416	3,000	240	1,305	.317

World Series

Year	G	AB	R	H	HR	RBI	Avg.
1960	7	29	1	9	0	3	.310
1971	7	29	3	12	2	4	.414

National League Playoffs

Year	G	AB	R	H	HR	RBI	Avg.
1969	3	14	1	3	0	1	.214
1970	4	18	2	6	0	4	.333
1972	5	17	1	4	1	2	.235

Major League All-Star Games

G	AB	R	H	HR	RBI	Avg.
14	31	3	10	1	4	.323

(Two games were played each season in 1960-61-62, one game each in 1963-64-65-66-67-69-70-71.)

PUERTO RICAN WINTER LEAGUE RECORD

(Played in 15 seasons)

AB	R	H	2B	3B	HR	RBI	Avg.
1,919	301	620	100	25	35	269	.323

(Santurce 1952-56; Caguas 1957-58, 1959-60; San Juan 1960-62, 1963-66, 1969-71)

Roberto began his career with the Santurce Crabbers.

With the Montreal Royals, 1954. It was a bad year.

Clemente goes high onto the rightfield wall to grab Dodger Pee Wee Reese's blast in game at Ebbets Field. July, 1955.

The Pirates, 1955. Left to right: Manager Bobby Bragan, Roberto Clemente, Dick Groat, Dale Long, Frank Thomas, Gene Freese, Toby Atwell, Bobby Del Greco, Johnny O'Brien, and Dick Hall.

Clemente was the first victim of a double play when Groat grounded out against the New York Giants at the Polo Grounds. May, 1955.

Roberto Clemente, Frank Thomas, Lee Walls, and Bill Virdon (left to right) were "big guns" of the Pirates in 1956.

Clemente scoots back safely to second on an attempted pickoff in game against the Dodgers, April, 1957. The Pirates won, 6-3.

Out at second on a force play in the first inning of a game against the Dodgers. August, 1960.

When rain postponed a game, Clemente visited the Phillies' dressing room. A wheelbarrow is a good lounge chair.

Roberto slides safely back to first as Phillies' first baseman leaps to snag the toss. June, 1960.

Heroes of the 1961 All-Star Game: Roberto Clemente, Pirates; Willie Mays, Giants; and Hank Aaron, Braves. The National League won, 5-4. Mays scored the winning run from second when Clemente singled to right field in the tenth inning.

Clemente climbs in a futile attempt to snare the San Francisco Giants' Hobie Landrith's 11th-inning homer. The Giants finally won in the 12th inning. April, 1961.

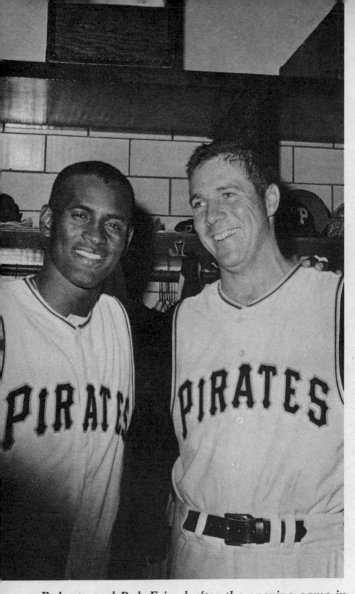

Roberto and Bob Friend after the opening game in 1962. Clemente hit a grand slam homer and Friend pitched a shutout against the Phillies. The Pirates won, 6-0.

In this 1962 game against the Dodgers, Clemente "waltzed" across the plate with pitcher John Podres. The dance began as Podres' pitch to home went wild. The catcher gave chase; Clemente was coming in to score, and Podres came in to block the plate. The catcher's throw was bad and bounced over the waltzers. Clemente scored, but the Dodgers won the game, 5-3.

Clemente snags the ball in the webbing of his glove after the Giants' Manny Mota hit deep to right. Mota was called out, although there was some argument as to whether Clemente dropped the ball. May, 1962.

Jim Gentile of the Orioles (left) and Clemente seem to be doing the twist in the 1962 All-Star Game. Actually Clemente was scrambling back to first to beat a pickoff.

Warren Giles, President of the National League, presents the Silver Bat, N.L. Batting Championship Award for 1961, to Roberto Clemente.

After grounding out with two men on, Roberto kicks his helmet. June, 1962.

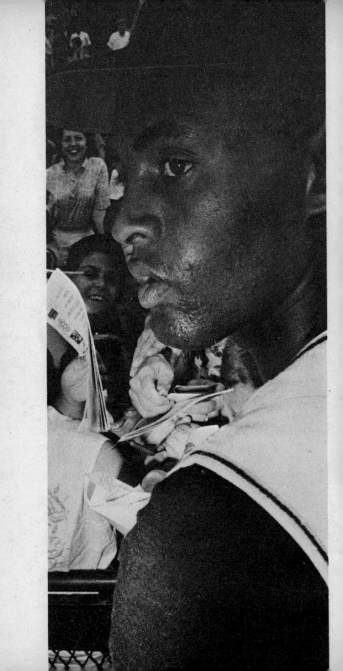

In a game against Cincinnati, Umpire Al Forman takes Clemente's bat from him, and draws a line over which Clemente is not to set foot. Roberto was persistently standing far back in the box. July, 1962.

Could I have your autograph please? The 1961 National League batting champion obliges.

Clemente steals second in a Cardinals-Pirates game, April, 1963. The Pirates won, 3-2.

Clemente steps back to first base as Phillies' first baseman Frank Thomas stretches for the pitcher's pickoff attempt. August, 1964.

In the eighth inning of a game on May 4, 1964, the Reds tried to hold Roberto on base with a throw to Deron Johnson. Clemente stole on the next pitch, and the Pirates won, 4-2.

Clemente tries for an inside-the-park home run, but Cincinnati catcher Johnny Edwards tags him out.

Never too busy for the fans. Signing autographs while on a visit to the New York World's Fair in 1964.

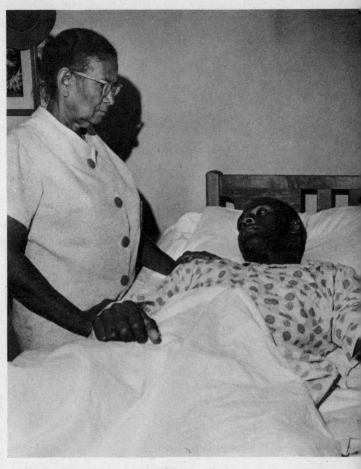

While recovering from malaria, Roberto gets an encouraging visit from his mother at Mimiya Hospital. March, 1965.

Warren Giles, President of the National League, presents the silver bat, N.L. Batting Championship Award for 1964, to Roberto Clemente.

Clemente is picked off at first base in a game with the Mets. Catcher Chris Cannizzaro threw to first base for the out. May, 1965.

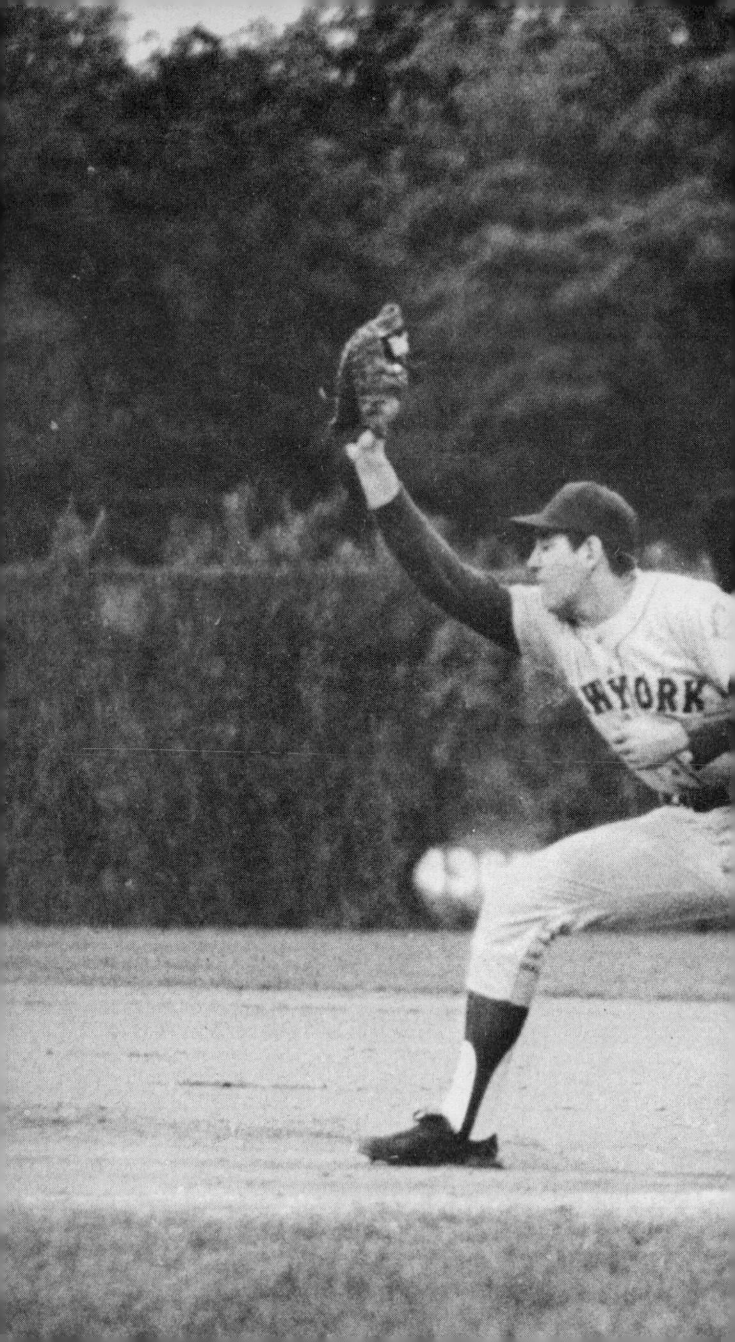
YORK

After hitting a bouncer, Clemente is out in close play at first by Mets' Ed Kranepool. June, 1965.

Clemente slides safely into third base after traveling from first on a hit by Stargell. The Pirates beat the Mets, 8-1.

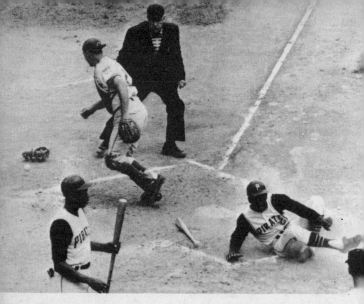

Clemente safe at home on Stargell's hit in a game against the Cubs, 1965.

Roberto breaks for first base in 1965 All-Star Game. The National League won, 6-5.

Roberto dodges a pitch thrown by Phil's Jim Bunning in a rough game. The Pirates won, 2-1.

Umpire Mel Steiner calls a strike in the first inning of a game with the Phillies. September 19, 1965.

Clemente makes it safely across the plate on an inside-the-park homer against the Cubs. Three runs scored on the play. July, 1966.

Roberto's 2,000th hit was a home run into the right-field stands in a game against the Chicago Cubs. Matty Alou congratulates him. September, 1966.

Roberto needed an ice pack on his neck on July 31, 1966, as the Pirates lost the first of three straight games to the Phillies, and lost the league lead as well.

*Clemente scores the tying run as the throw escapes
Cardinals' catcher Tim McCarver. Pirates won, 4-2.
September 9, 1967.*

The three top hitters in the N. L., July, 1967: (left to right) Tim McCarver of the Cards, Roberto Clemente of the Pirates, and Orlando Cepeda of the Cards.

Clemente reads his 1967 contract as General Manager Joe Brown looks on with approval. It was reported to be for around $100,000.

Roberto usually made the difficult catch look easy, but in this 1968 game against the Reds he outdid himself. Slipping in the muddy outfield while chasing Lee

May's fly ball, Roberto waits for the ball to come to him, gloves it and relaxes. Nevertheless, the Reds took the game, 8-2.

Roberto hitting Wrigley Field's ivy-covered right-field wall while trying for Chicago Cubs' Jim Hickman's triple, June 25, 1969. Clemente was shaken up in the play but continued in the game. Chicago won, 5-2.

In this 1969 game against the Cardinals, Roberto tries to score on a double by Stargell, but the ball got to Cards' catcher Tim McCarver just a second too soon.

Clemente with Danny Murtaugh. September, 1970.

Clemente stretches out to hit a single in the 7th inning of a game against the Giants. It was his 36th birthday—August 18, 1970.

Before "Roberto Clemente Night" at the Pitts-burgh stadium, Roberto indulges in a squeeze play with his son Rickie (Enrique).

Twisted around and in pain, Roberto pops a foul against the Mets, September 20, 1970. The play made Clemente's bad back worse, and he played very little for the rest of the season.

Roberto makes his point in a conversation at the start of the 1971 season.

The Clemente family at Shea Stadium in 1971. Roberto, holding son Enrique, greets his wife, Vera, and sons Roberto, Jr. (center) and Luis (right).

Clemente flying home as Cardinals' catcher Jerry McNertney waits for the throw. Roberto scored from second on Bob Robertson's single with the bases loaded.

Fierce traffic jam in Pirates-Giants game, October 3, 1971. At top left, Pirates' shortstop Hernandez (2) and centerfielder Clines (15) chase the ball. Both

missed it; it bounced high in the air. Bottom; Roberto has made it in from right field and snags the ball for the Pirates.

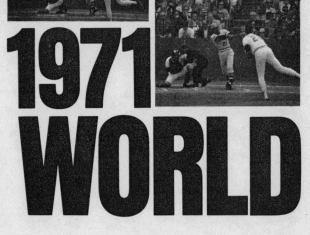

1971
WORLD

SERIES

Clemente and Nelson Briles are all smiles following the Pirates' 4-0 victory over the Orioles in the fifth game of the series. At this point Roberto was batting

.429 in the series. Briles collected the two-hit, complete game victory on October 14.

Roberto triples in the first inning of the sixth game. Pitching for the Orioles is Jim Palmer, catching is Elrod Hendricks.

The ball is headed for the rightfield stands as Roberto connects in the third inning of the sixth game. Orioles pitcher is Jim Palmer, catcher is Elrod Hendricks.

That grin says home run— Roberto is off to collect it.

Roberto makes note of the fact that Pittsburgh needs just one more victory to win the World Series.

In the seventh game, Roberto's fourth-inning homer gave the Pirates the lead that they never relinquished. Final score: 2-1 for the game, 4-3 for the series.

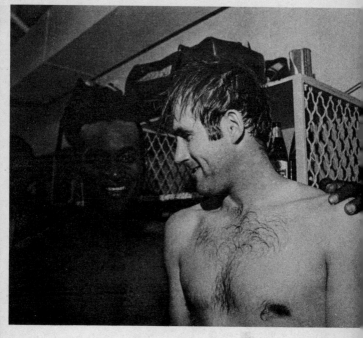

With Steve Blass—two wet World Champions.

In the dressing room after the seventh game: Roberto Clemente, star of the World Champion Pittsburgh Pirates.

1972

That beautiful batting action, captured by high-speed photography during spring training, 1972.

Roberto strains a knee on the first morning of full squad spring training.

Choosing a bat.

At bat against the Montreal Expos, May 19, 1972.

On September 30, 1972, Roberto hit No. 3,000. Umpire Doug Harvey hands him the ball as a keep-sake.

Willie Mays congratulates Roberto and welcomes him to the 3,000 hit club. Roberto is its 11th member.

*"The Great One" on base after his 3,000th+1 hit—
his first hit of the playoff. October 9, 1972.*

Roberto and Vera Clemente outside their home in Puerto Rico, December 15, 1972. As far as is known, this is the last picture of them together.

1973

New Year's Day, 1973. Searching in high seas.

A U.S. Navy diver among the shattered wreckage, 120 feet below the surface.

Watchers on the shore, New Year's Day.

Baseball Commissioner Bowie Kuhn (center) and Rodrigo Otero Suro, President of the Puerto Rican Baseball Winter League, after paying their respects to Mrs. Roberto Clemente. January 4, 1973.

After the ecumenical service for Clemente on January 14 in San Juan, Governor Rafael Hernandez Colon stops to have a word with the Clemente children. Mrs. Clemente holds a plaque presented to her during the service.

Trinity Cathedral, Pittsburgh: the memorial service for Roberto Clemente.

El 24 de julio de 1970, Los Piratas de Pittsburgh celebraron la Noche de Roberto Clemente, a la que asistieron 43,290 espectadores. El pelotero puertorriqueño logró dos hits en tres turnos al bate en esa noche suya, en que los Piratas aplastaron a los Astros de Houston con anotación de 11 por 0.

Después del juego alguien le preguntó a Roberto sobre el significado que la Noche había tenido para él.

"En un momento como éste—contestó Roberto— uno visualiza muchísimos años en sólo unos minutos. Uno ve que todo está firme y todo está claro.

"No sé si lloré, pero yo no me avergüenzo de llorar. Yo diría que un hombre nunca llora por dolor o por desilusión, pero si Usted conoce la historia de nuestra Isla, si conoce la forma en que nosotros somos criados, recordará que somos un pueblo sentimental.

"No tengo palabras para explicar cómo me siento al entrar al campo de juego sabiendo que hay tanta gente que me respalda . . . sabiendo que tantos son de mi Isla y de la América Latina."

La Víspera de Año Nuevo es noche de fiesta. Siempre ha sido así y continuará siéndolo, y la Noche de Año Viejo de 1972 habría sido igual a todas las demás. Cierto es que miles de personas habían muerto la semana previa, cuando un terremoto arrasó a Managua, la capital de Nicaragua. Y casi cien pasajeros perdieron la vida antes del inicio del neuvo año en un accidente aéreo en Miami.

Pero para casi todo el mundo esos fueron eventos distantes y la noche del 31 de diciembre del 1972 seguiría siendo la Víspera de Año Nuevo. Y para los peloteros del equipo Piratas de Pittsburgh era también noche de fiesta. En dicha ciudad Steve Blass, el lanzador estrella de la victoria Pirata en la Serie Mundial del 1971, y su compañero, el relevista Dave Giusti, celebraban la llegada del nuevo año.

Y Bob Johnson, Richie Zisk y Chuck Goggin, quienes jugaban beisbol invernal en Puerto Rico, celebraban también, en una fiesta que daba Johnson en su apartamento de un piso 27, desde donde se admiraba el Océano Atlántico en San Juan.

Pero un conocido Pirata no fiestaba esa noche. Roberto Clemente, el mejor y más famoso pelotero de Pittsburgh, había informado unos días antes que encabezaría la campaña de socorro para Managua y había empezado a colectar ropa y alimentos para las víctimas del terremoto. La noticia recibió poco espacio en los periódicos y muchos no prestaron mayor atención al asunto.

"Lo que hace es buscar publicidad—dijeron algunos—seguramente no hace nada, excepto dar su nombre y salir en los periódicos."

Los que así se expresaron no conocían a Clemente, quien nunca había permitido a nadie "usar su nombre." El super-astro boricua del beisbol ciertamente dirigía la campaña. La Víspera de Año Nuevo, en efecto, en el Aeropuerto Internacional de Isla Verde, cerca del apartamento de Johnson, Clemente supervisaba la carga de suministros para Nicaragua a bordo de un avión viejo de cuatro motores, tipo DC-7. El haría el viaje a la devastada capital centroamericana, para asegurarse de que la carga llegase a manos de las víctimas . . . y regresar luego a Puerto Rico para su propia celebración de Año Nuevo.

Pero las cosas no fueron bien en el aeropuerto. El avión tuvo problemas mecánicos y el piloto llegó tarde, por lo que la partida se retrasó un par de veces. Según alguien mencionó después, Clemente dijo: "Si hay otra demora dejaremos el viaje para mañana." Su esposa, Vera, se había preocupado porque el aparato lucía viejo y parecía estar sobrecargado. Roberto le dijo: "Todo va a salir bien, por lo tanto me voy. Eso sí, asegúrate de tener lechoncito asado para mí y los nenes cuando regrese."

En el apartamento de Johnson, Richie Zisk dijo luego: "Oímos decir que un avión se había estrellado . . . Vimos a los equipos de rescate salir en busca de los cadáveres con enormes proyectores de luz y hablamos sobre la terrible situación de los pasajeros, pero no teníamos idea del tipo de avión que sería. Y platicamos sobre lo trágico que resultaría el Día de Año Nuevo para los familiares y amigos de las víctimas."

Chuck Goggin recordó que un amigo había tratado de convencer a Roberto de no hacer el viaje. Y éste presuntamente le dijo: "Bueno, ya me voy. Si me toca morir . . . moriré."

Eran las cuatro de la madrugada en Pittsburgh cuando sonó el teléfono en la fiesta de Steve Blass y Dave Giusti. Llamaba Tony Bartirome, entrenador de los Piratas, que había oído la noticia por radio. Y casi a la misma hora Joe L. Brown, gerente general del equipo y amigo y confidente de Roberto, fue despertado por el teléfono. Poco después Blass y Giusti llegaban a la casá de Brown, el único lugar adonde se les ocurrió ir en esos momentos.

La fiesta había terminado . . . todas las fiestas habían terminado.

La súbita muerte de Roberto Clemente probablemente haya sido sentida por más personas, en más formas diferentes, que la de cualquier astro deportivo durante muchos años. Ciertamente hay peloteros que triunfan y peloteros que fracasan. Hay muchos que se retiran del deporte al final de sus carreras y otros que pasan a mejor vida. Pero desde Lou Gehrig, nadie de la magnitud de Clemente, aun en la era apoteósica de su carrera, ha tenido un final tan trágico.

"Si es que uno tiene que morir—dijo el propietario de los Piratas, John W. Galbreath—¿hay forma más simbólica que durante una misión piadosa? Ese era el tipo de hombre que era Roberto."

Sin duda. Esa era, sin embargo, una de las personalidades de Clemente que poca gente conocía, incluyendo a sus compañeros de equipo. A la mayor parte de ellos les sorprendió que el astro puertorriqueño estuviese envuelto en la campaña de socorro para Nicaragua, y muchos se enteraron al enterarse de su deceso.

Para el público Clemente era un hombre multifacético . . . complejo. Algunos lo consideraban un hipocondriaco, que no hacía más que quejarse de presuntas lesiones. "Yo no aguanto al tipo—dijo el doctor Joseph Finegold, médico de los Piratas, cuando Clemente voló una vez a Puerto Rico para ser atendido por su médico personal—y si vuelve adonde mí a quejarse de sus dolamas . . . le diré que vaya a curarse a Puerto Rico. Y se lo contaré a Joe Brown."

Brown, gerente general del equipo, no aceptó la idea de que Roberto se quejara por el gusto. "La verdad es—dijo Brown—que aun cuando está enfermo Roberto juega mejor que la mayor parte de nuestros hombres cuando están perfectamente sanos."

Algunos veían en Clemente al "hombre de las protestas" . . . un individuo que según él nunca había recibido el reconocimiento merecido. En 1960, creyendo que había sido el jugador más valioso de la Liga Nacional, alegó que se le debió haber otorgado dicho trofeo, que fue ganado por otro pelotero. Fue esa una de las razones por las cuales muchos lo consideraban un hombre petulante. Pero nadie podía negarle que era un astro.

Quizá Roberto hubiese pasado su vida de pelotero sin que se apreciaran sus talentos, pero él sabía lo mucho que valía y lo decía claramente: "Para mí, yo soy el mejor de todos." Y al final de la Serie Mundial del 71, después de 17 años en las Mayores, el super-astro boricua recibió por fin el reconocimiento nacional que lo colocó a la altura de las más grandes estrellas en la historia del deporte.

Aparte de su indiscutible habilidad como pelotero, había un extraordinario ser humano dentro de Roberto Clemente.

Sólo sus más íntimos conocían sus labores de caridad; su sueño de construir una Ciudad Deportiva para la muchachada puertorriqueña; su deseo de ayudar a la niñez y al pueblo; su gran lucha por los peloteros latinoamericanos . . . y su genuino interés por la igualdad racial. Como ejemplo, el pago que recibía por anuncios comerciales de radio, prensa o televisión hechos por Clemente en Puerto Rico, era donado a obras de caridad. Y los 6,000 dólares que le tocaron por la Noche de Roberto Clemente en el Three Rivers Stadium en 1970, fueron donados al Hospital de Niños de Pittsburgh.

Pero a pesar de todo su controversial personalidad provocaba una reacción ambivalente de parte del público, que demandaba que él jugase siempre en forma brillante, cosa que él hacía. Tal actuación sin embargo, no evitaba las críticas. Por eso Roberto se crecía constantemente al ponerse el uniforme. Y además se crecía también en sus obras de caridad, que en la mayor parte de los casos no recibían publicidad alguna, porque así lo quería él. Eso sí, continuaba siempre diciendo lo que sentía sobre todo y sobre todos, criticando o aplaudiendo a los cronistas deportivos, a los fanáticos, a los umpires, a los peloteros de otros equipos, a los managers . . . y hasta a sus propios compañeros Piratas. No hay duda de que era controversial, pero era casi imposible no quererlo.

Así, casi todas las personas con quienes tuvo contacto dentro del beisbol lo recuerdan con respeto, sino también con cariño. Steve Blass dijo al enterarse de su muerte: "Cuando pienso en lo interesante que es nuestro deporte, pienso en Roberto Clemente. Su influencia permanecerá con nosotros por largo tiempo—es más, es difícil pensar en los Piratas de Pittsburgh sin Roberto Clemente."

La lista de galardones recibidos por él en las Grandes Ligas es sin duda altamente impresionante.

—Fue campeón de bateo de la Liga Nacional en 1961, 1964, 1965 y 1967. Y casi ganó otras dos veces, como en 1968, cuando Pete Rose lo venció con una planchita en su última vez al bate en la temporada.

—En 1966 fue el Pelotero Más Valioso de la Liga.

—En 1972 bateó su hit número 3,000, hazaña lograda tan sólo por otros 10 peloteros de las dos Ligas en los casi 100 años de historia del del Deporte.

—Jugó en más partidos, tuvo más turnos al bate, más hits, más sencillos y empujó más carreras que ningún otro hombre en la historia de los Piratas.

—Ganó el Guante de Oro por eficiencia en fildeo

en cada uno de los últimos 12 años.

—Su promedio al bate para toda su carrera fue de .317.

Sobre todo eso, valga decir que Roberto será más recordado como el Jugador Más Valioso de Pittsburgh en la Serie Mundial de 1971, cuando bateó .414, logró hits en cada uno de los siete juegos y pegó un jonrón al principio del séptimo, en que los Piratas alcanzaron la victoria. Hizo todo eso, además de actuar brillantemente al campo y reservar suficiente tiempo para tener una controversia con el gran pelotero de Baltimore Frank Robinson.

Al final de ese juego el magnífico ser humano que era Clemente, al ser entrevistado al micrófono en su camerino, aprovechó la ocasión para decir unas palabras en español para sus padres en Puerto Rico. "En éste, el momento en que más orgullo he sentido en mi vida, les pido a ustedes la Bendición," dijo Roberto.

Nacido en Río Piedras el 18 de agosto de 1934, fue uno de cuatro hermanos, uno de los cuales, Justino, jugaba beisbol aficionado y posiblemente hubiera sido un buen profesional, pero al regresar del servicio militar en la guerra de Corea, aparentemente sus habilidades decayeron. Pero Roberto continuaba jugando regularmente y un día pegó 10 jonrones en el mismo partido.

En una de sus últimas entrevistas, recordando esa niñez, él señaló: "Yo era feliz poruque mi mamá y mi papá, y mis hermanos, nos sentábamos al anochecer en la casa y hablábamos y hacíamos chistes . . . y comíamos lo que hubiese. Eso era maravilloso para mí, pues todos teníamos que luchar mucho para tener qué comer. Y cuando era más difícil encontrar alimentos, nuestros padres nos daban primero a nosotros y ellos comían lo que sobraba. Ellos vivían sólo para nosotros . . . para darnos felicidad."

Además de jugar beisbol, practicar otros deportes y adquirir una educación, el futuro astro también trabajaba . . . repartiendo leche a las seis de la mañana en las casas de la vecindad, antes de ir a la escuela. El muchachito llevaba una gran vasija llena de leche, pesada y difícil de cargar, pero no se quejaba. "Después de todo—dijo en una ocasión—me ganaba un centavo diario, de manera que a fin de mes tenía 30 o 31 chavos. Y a los tres años había ahorrado suficiente para comprarme una bicicleta de segunda mano que me costó 27 pesos."

Otros de sus más interesantes recuerdos de esa época, María Isabel Cáceres, era maestra de historia de la escuela superior Julio Vizcarrondo de Carolina. Roberto era para ella un jovencito humilde y callado "a quien tengo que recordar con gran cariño —afirmó doña María Isabel—porque una vez, en el año 1962 cuando ya era un famoso y muy bien pagado pelotero, fue a verme a mi casa, donde yo estaba en cama por una lesión en la espalda y apenas podía moverme. Roberto me levantó en brazos y me llevó a un médico. Y así lo hizo todos los días hasta que pude caminar."

En sus años de escuela superior fue el Jugador Más Valioso del equipo de beisbol por tres años corridos. Y era también bueno en deportes de pista y campo. Por ejemplo, lanzaba la javalina hasta 195 pies, en el salto alto llegó a los seis pies y en triple salto brincó 45, magníficas actuaciones para un atleta de escuela superior.

A los 18 años se presentó con un guante raído al

parque de los Cangrejeros de Santurce, equipo profesional de la Liga Invernal Puertorriqueña, y practicó con ellos en el Jardín Corto. Pedrín Zorrilla, el propietario del equipo, le dijo: "Puedes empezar ya a jugar con nosotros," ofreciéndole 500 dólares y un guante nuevo. Roberto firmó y se convirtió en profesional, bateando .234 en la primera temporada, con 18 hits en 77 turnos al bate. En las tres próximas, sin embargo, logró promedios de .288, .344 y .306. Y continuó jugando en la Liga Puertorriqueña todos los inviernos, aún después de haberse graduado a las Mayores.

El manager del Santurce, Buck Clarkson, dijo al principio de la carrera de Clemente, "algún día será tan bueno como Willie Mays." Y así ocurrió.

En el año 1953 el escucha Al Campanis, de los Dodgers de Brooklyn, seleccionó a Roberto de entre 72 jóvenes peloteros puertorriqueños que practicaron para él en el Estadio Sixto Escobar. Recordó Campanis: "Lo primero que pedí a los muchachos fue que tirasen la pelota desde los bosques . . . y aquel jovencito la disparaba como si fuera una bala. Le pedí que volviera a tirar y lo hizo mejor todavía. Quedé maravillado. Luego dije a los jóvenes que corrieran 60 yardas. Clemente lo hizo en 6.4 segundos. No podía creerlo y le pedí que volviera a hacerlo. Efectivamente, 6.4 otra vez, de manera que envié a los otros candidatos a sus casas y me quedé con Roberto.

"Lo puse entonces a batear y me convencí de que tenía a un fenómeno que le pegaba a cualquier lanzamiento. Decidí firmarlo, pero como estaba aún en la escuela superior, el reglamento no le permitía, así que tuve que regresar a Brooklyn sin él," terminó diciendo Campanis.

Pero el próximo año, ya fuera de la escuela, los Dodgers le ofrecieron 10,000 pesos y Clarkson recomendó que los aceptase, aunque los Bravos, entonces en Milwaukee, le habian ofrecido 35,000. Clarkson lo convenció al decirle que todos los peloteros de los Dodgers eran amigos suyos y que él les pediría que lo ayudasen.

Su carrera en el Norte empezó con el Montreal, equipo de las Menores de Brooklyn, debido a que en los bosques tenía a Jackie Robinson, bateando .329; a Duke Snider, con promedio de .336 y a Carl Furillo, con .344. En otras palabras, no había espacio para un novato llamado Roberto Clemente. Pero como el sueldo que se le había pagado era suficientemente alto los Dodgers, de acuerdo al reglamento, tenían que subirlo al equipo de las Grandes Ligas o ponerlo en el "draft," para dar a los otros equipos la oportunidad de comprar su contrato.

Brooklyn no quería que Roberto fuera comprado por los Gigantes, entonces en Nueva York, y con Willie Mays en el bosque central. Y Clemente y Mays en el equipo rival de Brooklyn hubieran representado demasiado peligro. Por eso se hizo una campaña para mantener a Roberto en el banco, poniéndolo a jugar muy raramente, para que los Gigantes no se enterasen de que había un gran prospecto al otro lado del río que podría ser comprado por muy poco.

Como es natural Clemente estaba desilusionado, pues sólo apareció en 87 juegos en 1954, bateando .257 y emujando sólo 12 carreras. "Pero todo el mundo sabía de lo que yo era capaz, pues antes de firmar con Brooklyn había ocho equipos de las Mayores detrás de mí. Por lo tanto, yo estaba seguro de que me perderían en el draft," pensó Roberto.

Los Piratas en esos dias estaban terminando la temporada en el sótano de la Nacional, lo que les daba la oportunidad de seleccionar primero en el draft. Su primer interés era Joe Black, un magnífico pitcher que los Dodgers habían enviado a Montreal. El escucha Clyde Sukeforth fue enviado a Richmond (Virginia), donde Montreal estaba jugando. "Llegué justo a tiempo para ver a los hombres practicando antes del juego—dijo Clyde—y Clemente estaba tirando la pelota desde los bosques. Quedé maravillado. Luego, en el partido, lo usaron como bateador de emergencia y me gustó la forma en que lo hizo. Al preguntar me enteré que estaría en el draft."

Pittsburgh compró al fenómeno boricua por sólo 4,000 dólares, comenzando Clemente su carrera en las Ligas Mayores.

De ahí en adelante el pelotero puertorriqueño se convirtió en uno de los más extraordinarios astros en la historia del beisbol. Su compleja personalidad, sin embargo, le creó tantas dificultades como su habilidad en el campo de juego le produjo aplausos . . . y aumentos de salario. Sí, Roberto alcanzó el codiciado nivel en que se le llegó a pagar hasta 100,000 pesos al año . . . y eventualmente fue reconocido como líder por sus compañeros de equipo.

Pero no fue todo rosas. Roberto siempre fue un hombre honrado, que siempre dijo valientemente lo que sentía, bueno o malo, respecto a todo lo que tenía que ver con el deporte. Eso, como es natural, le ganó enemigos, muchos de los cuales más tarde llegaron a quererlo. En muchos casos fue él mismo quien se retractó por haber dicho algo que luego consideró injusto. En otras ocasiones los individuos comprendieron que el super-astro boricua tenía razón en los conceptos emitidos.

Clemente coninuó distinguiéndose en los campos de beisbol hasta el último momento, y luchando intensamente por los derechos de los jugadores latinoamericanos y de color. La mayor parte de sus compañeros de equipo llegaron a considerarlo un gran amigo. Y sus compatriotas, así como los ciudadanos miembros de minorías, siempre lo tuvieron como gran defensor.

Ejemplo claro de su forma de pensar y actuar fue un incidente ocurrido en Nueva York, en ocasión de ir a comprar muebles. Roberto, que había contraído matrimonio con la bellísima Vera Christina Zabala el 14 de noviembre de 1963 en Carolina (Puerto Rico), fue a la mueblería con ella. Al llegar a la tienda, según dijo Roberto después, un hombre los recibió en forma poco amable diciendo: "¿Qué quieren ustedes?"

Clemente respondió: "Nos gustaría ver algunos muebles." El individuo les dijo que esperasen, que mandaría a alguien a llevarlos al último piso, donde estaban los que a ellos les gustarían. En el camino Roberto y Vera lograron ver una elegante sala de exhibición, con muebles superiorísimos a los del último piso y le dijo al hombre que preferirían ver aquéllos que, según dijo el vendedor, eran muy caros.

Clemente dijo entonces: "Pues yo quiero verlos, porque tengo ese derecho. Yo soy un ser humano que viene a comprar aquí."

Al fin de la discusión el hombre los llevó a la sala

y Roberto, que en esos días preparaba un viaje a Europa y tenía 5,000 dólares en la billetera, sacó la plata y dijo hombre: "¿Cree usted que con ésto podríamos comprar algunos de estos muebles?" Y entonces quisieron mostrarles todo lo que tenían en existencia. El vendedor exclamó: "Creíamos que ustedes eran como todo los demás puertorriqueños."

Y eso molestaba de verdad a Clemente, que por ser puertorriqueño se le tratase en forma diferente. Así que, puso la billetera en el bolsillo, y salieron de la mueblería sin comprar nada.

Sin duda el super-astro boricua era un gran luchador en cualquier campo de importancia para los seres humanos. Pero al ponerse el uniforme Pirata, iba al campo de juego a dar todo su potencial. Y el año recientemente pasado logró su hit número 3,000 . . . en forma tan compleja como el pelotero complejo que era.

La noche del 29 de septiembre de 1972, 24,193 fanáticos fueron al estadio a ver a los Piratas confrontar a los Mets de Nueva York, con Tom Seaver lanzando. La noche anterior el boricua había bateado su incogible número 2,999.

En su primer turno, al final del primer inning, Roberto bateó por sobre el montículo y el segunda base, Ken Boswell, tuvo oportunidad de sacarlo out. Pero mofó la pelota, llegando a primera base el boricua. El anotador oficial anunció en el palco de la prensa: "Error por el segunda base . . . Error por Boswell." Pero los que trabajaban en la pizarra eléctrica no lo oyeron y no lo carcaron. Los espectadores comenzaron a aplaudir, pero al rato se marcó el error en la pizarra—Clemente no había bateado hit. El boricua se enfureció y dijo: "Toda mi vida me han robado . . . Me lo hacen a cada rato. Por el hecho de que yo digo lo que siento sobre ellos, me roban muchos hits."

Pero al rato se calmó y dijo: "De todas formas, es preferible que el incogible sea limpio."

Y al otro día, el 30 de septiembre, lo logró. Era sábado y, a las 3:07 de la tarde, en Pittsburgh, el pitcher de los Mets Jon Matlack—que luego fue nombrado Novato del Año de la Liga Nacional— lanzó una curva a Clemente en el cuarto inning, que el boricua bateó hacia la brecha izquierda del bosque central, convirtiéndos en doble. Fue ese su hit número 3.000 . . . y el último de su vida en una temporada regular.

Tres meses después Roberto Clemente había muerto.

Calces de las Fotografías

p. 60   *Roberto al comienzo de su carrera con los Cangrejeros de Santurce.*

p. 61   *Con los Reales de Montreal, 1954. El año no fue bueno.*

p. 62   *Piratas de 1955. De izquierda a derecha: El manager Bobby Bragan, Roberto Clemente, Dick Groat, Dale Long, Frank Thomas, Gene Freese, Toby Atwell, Bobby del Greco, Johnny O'Brien y Dick Hall.*

p. 63   *Clemente se eleva en la cerca del bosque derecho para atrapar batazo de Pee Wee Reese en juego en Ebbets Field (Brooklyn) en julio de 1955.*

p. 64   *Clemente resulta primera víctima de doble-matanza al roletear Groat contra los Gigantes de Nueva York en Polo Grounds, en mayo de 1955.*

p. 65   *Roberto Clemente, Frank Thomas, Lee Walls y Bill Virdon, (izquierda a derecha) cañoneros de los Piratas en 1956.*

p. 66-67   *Clemente corre de regreso a segunda cuando los Dodgers trataban de sacarlo out en juego en abril, 1957. Los Piratas ganaron, por 6-3.*

p. 68   *Roberto out en segunda en jugada forzada en primer inning de juego contra Brooklyn en agosto de 1960.*

p. 69   *En juego pospuesto por lluvia Clemente visita el camerino de los Filis; una carretilla se convierte en silla de descanso.*

p. 70   *Roberto regresa de slide a primera, mientras primera base de los Filis trata de tocarlo para ponerlo out. Junio de 1960.*

p. 71   *Héroes del Juego de las Estrellas de 1961: Roberto Clemente, Piratas; Willie Mays, Gigantes y Hank Aaron, Bravos. La Liga Nacional ganó por 5-4. Mays anotó la carrera ganadora desde segunda cuando Clemente bateó sencillo al bosque derecho en el décimo inning.*

p. 72-73   Clemente en intento inútil de parar jonrón en undécimo inning de Hobie Landrith, de los Gigantes de San Francisco. Los Gigantes ganaron en el 12mo. Abril de 1961.

p. 74   Roberto y Bob Friend después de primer juego de 1962. Clemente cañoneó un jonrón con las bases llenas y Friend lanzó un partido sin carreras contra los Filis. Los Piratas ganaron por 6-0.

p. 75   En juego contra los Dodgers en 1962 Clemente "bailó" sobre el plato con el pitcher Johnny Podres. El asunto comenzó cuando Podres hizo un mal lanzamiento y el receptor corrió tras de la bola. Clemente venía a anotar y Podres corrió a cubrir el plato. La tirada del catcher también fue mala, rebotando sobre los "bailarines". Roberto anotó.

p. 76-77   Clemente atrapa la pelota en el calado de su guante, al pegar Many Mota, de los Gigantes, un largo batazo al bosque derecho. Mota fue declarado out, aunque hubo discusión sobre si Roberto dejó caer la bola. Mayo de 1962.

p. 78   Jim Gentile, de los Orioles (Izq.), y Clemente parecen estar bailando el twist en el Juego de las Estrellas de 1962. Lo que hacía Roberto era correr de regreso a primera para evitar salir out.

p. 79   (abajo) Luego de salir out con dos hombres en base, Roberto patea su protector. Junio, 1962.

p. 79   (arriba) Warren Giles, presidente de la Liga Nacional, extrega el Bate de Plata, trofeo del Campeonato de Bateo de la Liga, en 1961 a Roberto Clemente.

p. 80   ¿Me da su autógrafo?—El campeón bate del 1961 de la Liga Nacional lo hace con gusto.

p. 81   En juego contra Cincinnati el umpire Al Forman quita el bate a Clemente y traza una línea, más allá de la cual Roberto no podrá poner los pies. El boricua persistentemente se paraba a batear muy detrás del plato. Julio de 1962.

p. 82-83   *Clemente roba segunda en juego entre Piratas y Cardenales, abril de 1963. Los Piratas ganaron, 3-2.*

p. 84-85   *Roberto regresa a primera mientras Frank Thomas, primera base de los Filis, se estira para racibir la pelota tirada por el pitcher, en intento de sacarlo out. Agosto, 1964.*

p. 86-87   *En octavo inning de juego del cuatro de mayo de 1964, los Rojos tratan de mantener en base a Roberto con tirada a Deron Johnson. Clemente robó en próximo lanzamiento del pitcher y los Piratas vencieron por 4-2.*

p. 88-89   *Roberto trata de anotar jonrón dentro del parque, pero Johnny Edwards, receptor de Cincinnati, lo pone out.*

p. 90   *Clemente firma autógrafos en visita a la Feria Mundial de Nueva York, en 1964.*

p. 91   *Recobrándose de un ataque de malaria, Roberto recibe visita de su mamá en la Clínica Mimiya. Marzo de 1965.*

p. 92   *Warren Giles, presidente de la Liga Nacional, entrega el Bate de Plata, trofeo del Campeonato de Bateo de la Liga, en 1964, a Roberto Clemente.*

p. 93   *Clemente sale out en primera base en juego contra los Mets de Nueva York. El catcher, Cannizzaro, tiró a primera para hacer el out.*

p. 94-95   *Clemente es out en primera, en difícil jugada por Ed Kranepool, luego de batear rola saltarina en juego contra los Mets en junio de 1965.*

p. 96-97   *Clemente llega a tercera de slide, corriendo desde primera con hit de Stargell. Los Piratas ganaron, por 8-1.*

p. 98   *(abajo) Roberto corriendo hacia primera en Juego de Estrellas de 1965. La Liga Nacional se impuso con anotación de 6-5.*

p. 98   *(arriba) Clemente anota con hit de Stargell en juego contra los Cubs de Chicago, 1965.*

p. 99   Roberto evade pelotazo en lanzamiento del pitcher Jim Bunning, de los Filis de Filadelfia, en un juego que los Piratas ganaron por 2-1, el 29 de septiembre de 1966.

p. 100-101   Umpire Mel Steiner declara strike en primer inning de juego contra los Filis, septiembre 1965.

p. 102-103   Clemente llega al plato con jonrón dentro del parque en juego contra los Cubs, produciendo tres carreras. Julio, 1966.

p. 104   Roberto con bolsa de hielo en cuello, julio 31 de 1966, al perder los Piratas el primero de tres juegos consecutivos, perdiendo también la delantera en la Liga Nacional.

p. 105   El hit número 2,000 de Clemente fue un jonrón en la gradería del bosque derecho, en juego contra los Cubs, en septiembre, 1966. Matty Alou lo felicita.

p. 106-107   Clemente anota carrera empatadora al perder la pelota el catcher Cardenal, Tim McCarver, en juego de septiembre 9, 1967. Los Piratas ganaron, 4-2.

p. 108   Los tres bateadores en la delantera en la Liga Nacional, en julio de 1967. De izquierda a derecha: Tim McCarver, Cardenales; y los puertorriqueños Roberto Clemente, Piratas, y Orlando Cepeda, Cardenales.

p. 109   Roberto leyendo su contrato de 1967 mientras el gerente de los Piratas, Joe Brown, observa con aprobación. Según se informó, el salario fue de alrededor de 100.000 pesos.

p. 110-111   Regularmente Clemente hacía que las más difíciles cogidas apareciesen fáciles, pero en este juego contra los Rojos en 1968, su actuación fue aún más extraordinaria. Dando un resbalón en el mojado terreno mientras corría hacia el lugar donde esperaba que bajase la pelota, Roberto espera por ella, la recibe en el guante y luego descansa. De todas formas, los Rojos ganaron el juego con anotación de 8-2.

p. 112-113   *Clemente choca contra la pared del bosque derecho de Wrigley Field (Chicago), en su carrera para atrapar el triple de Jim Hickman, de los Cubs, el 25 de junio de 1969. Roberto sufrió una buena sacudida pero permaneció en el juego. Chicago venció, por 5-2.*

p. 114-115   *En juego contra los Cardenales en 1969, Roberto trata de anotar con un doble de Stargell, pero el receptor Tim McCarver recibió la bola justo a tiempo para ponerlo out.*

p. 116-117   *Clemente en compañía de Danny Murtaugh, septiembre de 1970.*

p. 118-119   *Clemente batea sencillo en el séptimo inning de juego contra los Gigantes el 18 de agosto de 1970, día en que cumplió 36 años.*

p. 120   *Antes de la Noche de Roberto Clemente, celebrada en el estadio de Pittsburgh, el astro puertorriqueño juega con su hijo Rickie (Enrique).*

p. 121   *Clemente, transido de dolor, sale out al batear foul en juego contra los Mets, el 20 de septiembre de 1970. El esfuerzo agravó la lesión que tenía en la espalda, permitiéndole jugar muy poco en el resto de la temporada.*

p. 122   *Roberto conversa con compañeros al principio de la temporada de 1971.*

p. 123   *La familia Clemente visita Shea Stadium (Nueva York), en 1971. Roberto tiene a Enrique mientras saluda a su esposa Vera y sus hijos Roberto, Junior (centro), y Luis (derecha).*

p. 124-125   *Clemente "vuela" mientras el catcher Cardenal, Jerry McNertney, espera por la bola. Roberto anotó desde segunda con sencillo de Bob Robertson con las bases llenas.*

p. 126-127   *Arriba, izquierda. En juego entre Piratas y Dodgers el 3 de octubre de 1971, el shortstop Pirata Hernández (2) y el guardabosque central Clines (15), pierden la pelota. Abajo, Roberto, corriendo desde el bosque derecho, la agarra en el rebote.*

p. 130-131 *Clemente y Nelson Briles sonríen luego de la victoria Pirata sobre los Orioles por 4-0, en el quinto juego de la Serie Mundial. A esas alturas Roberto estaba bateando .429 en la serie y Briles había ganado el partido, permitiendo sólo dos hits. Octubre, 14.*

p. 132-133 *Roberto cañonea triple en sexto juego. Por los Orioles lanzó Jim Palmer y el catcher fue Elrod Hendricks.*

p. 134 *La pelota vuela hacia las graderías detrás del bosque derecho. en jonrón de Clemente en el tercer inning del sexto partido. Por los Orioles seguía lanzando Jim Palmer, y Hendricks seguía recibiendo.*

p. 135 *Roberto sonríe al disparar el jonrón.*

p. 136 *Clemente indica que a los Piratas sólo les falta una victoria para ganar la Serie Mundial.*

p. 137 *En el séptimo juego, Roberto pegó jonrón en el cuarto inning, dando ventaja a los Piratas que nunca perdieron. La anotación final fue 2-1, dando la victoria a Pittsburgh por cuatro juegos a tres.*

p. 138 *En el camerino después del séptimo juego, Roberto Clemente, astro Pirata de la Serie.*

p. 139 *Clemente y Steve Blass.*

p. 141 *Octubre de 1972—Clemente recibe a jovencitos puertorriqueños en el nuevo estadio Three Rivers.*

p. 142 *Belleza del estilo de bateo de Roberto Clemente, capturada por foto de alta velocidad durante entrenamiento de primavera, 1972.*

p. 143 *Roberto sufre lesión en rodilla en primer día de Entrenamiento de Primavera.*

p. 144 *Escogiendo bate.*

p. 145 *Al bate contra los Expos de Montreal, mayo 19, 1972.*

p. 146-147 *Septiembre 30 de 1972: Umpire Doug Harvey entrega a Roberto pelota que bateó en el hit número 3,000.*

p. 148 *Willie Mays felicita a Roberto y let da la bien-venida al Club de los 3,000 Hits. Roberto es el número 11.*

p. 149 *El Super-Astro en base luego de su hit número 3,001, el primero en la serie de "playoff," octubre 9, 1972.*

p. 150 *Roberto y Vera Clemente frente a su hogar en Puerto Rico. Hasta donde se sabe, esta fue la última tomada de los dos.*

p. 154-155 *Día de Año Nuevo, 1973. Búsqueda de cadáveres en el mar.*

p. 156 *(arriba) Buzo de la Marina entre los escombros, a 120 pies de profundidad. Una sección del fuselaje del avión, de 75 pies, quedó hecha pedazos.*

p. 156 *(abajo) Público espera en la playa el día de Año Nuevo, mientras continúa la búsqueda.*

p. 157 *El Comisionado de Beisbol, Bowie Kuhn (centro), y el Lcdo. Rodrigo Otero Suro, presidente de la Liga Puertorriqueña de Beisbol, parten de la residencia de Clemente, luego de presentar sus condolencias a la viuda. Cuatro de enero de 1973.*

p. 158 *Luego del servicio ecuménico en honor a Clemente el 14 de enero en San Juan, el gobernador Rafael Hernández Colón conversa con los huérfanos hijos de Clemente. La viuda, Vera Zabala de Clemente, sostiene la placa recibida durante el servicio.*

p. 159 *Catedral de la Trinidad (Pittsburgh)—Servicio en memoria de Roberto Clemente.*